# 150 Best Sustainable House Ideas

# 150 Best Sustainable House Ideas

HARPER
DESIGN

*An Imprint of HarperCollinsPublishers*

150 BEST SUSTAINABLE HOUSE IDEAS
Copyright © 2013 by HARPER DESIGN and LOFT Publications

First published in 2013 by:
Harper Design
*An Imprint of* HarperCollins*Publishers*
10 East 53rd Street
New York, NY 10022
Tel.: (212) 207-7000
Fax: (212) 207-7654
harperdesign@harpercollins.com
www.harpercollins.com

Distributed throughout the world by:
HarperCollins*Publishers*
10 East 53rdStreet
New York, NY 10022
Fax: (212) 207-7654

Editorial coordinator: Claudia Martínez Alonso
Art director: Mireia Casanovas Soley
Editor and texts: Francesc Zamora Mola
Graphic editor: Manel Gutiérrez (@mgutico)
Layout: Cristina Simó Perales
Cover layout: Emma Termes Parera

ISBN: 978-0-06-231549-6

Library of Congress Control Number: 2013954401

Printed in China
First printing, 2013

# Contents

# Introduction

Interest in sustainable architecture is increasing as people become more concerned with the deteriorating environment and dwindling fossil fuel supplies. In residential architecture, as in any other building category, measurement tools have triggered changes in the design process, and these changes are in turn changing construction methods.

Around the world, environmental and energy-efficiency concerns are being addressed by institutions such as the United States Green Building Council (USGBC), the creator of the LEED (Leadership in Energy and Environmental Design) requirements for sustainable buildings, and BREEAM (Building Research Establishment's Environmental Assessment Method) established in the UK. The requirements not only focus on energy use but also on issues such as water efficiency, carbon emissions, and materials use, all with the goal of improving environmental quality.

The types of environmentally friendly construction measures are continuously being upgraded in response to an ever-worsening environmental situation and rising energy costs. There seems to be a growing movement towards net-zero buildings—buildings that have zero net energy consumption and zero carbon emissions annually. Over the years, rules for building homes have changed, and today it is no longer acceptable to design without considering the context of the location. Houses need to respond to their immediate environment in order to reach quality efficiency levels.

The design process for sustainable homes starts with a series of questions: How is the building going to respond to the site's orientation, wind exposure, and solar gain? How will it maximize natural light? How can the builders reduce construction waste? How can the house provide heating and cooling with a minimum production of $CO_2$?

In order to achieve sustainable goals, buildings can no longer be a composition of different systems. Rather, they need to be conceived as an integrated whole with building elements, including the structure, mechanical equipment, and materials, strongly connected to each other and serving more than one function. For instance, the structure may not only support its loads, but may also serve as a heat sink for passive heating and cooling.

The effort to maximize sustainability does not end when a building is complete. Humans need to see a sustainable building as a living structure that is part of a larger good, and encourage their communities to be environmentally conscious.

This project was born out of the remnants of a Robin Gibson cottage that existed on the site. The design, inspired by the work of both Gibson and architect Richard Neutra, is a contemporary reinterpretation of modernist design. The house enjoys a long, linear plan with the rooms arranged to soak up the winter sun. A natural palette of zinc, tallow wood, slate, and travertine creates a robust and timeless aesthetic.

## One Wybelenna

Architects: Shaun Lockyer
Architects
Location: Brookfield, Brisbane,
Australia
Photography: © Scott Burrows

The structural method, stone masonry, and landscape are key aspects of the design and were considered from the outset, as was the environmental design strategy.

## 001

The environmental, economic, and aesthetic benefits of green roofs are widely recognized. These benefits include the protection of waterproofing, water retention, and thermal insulation.

The new guest pavilion sits on the
original footprint of the Gibson cottage
and reuses the original stone. The
planning of the house prioritizes solar
orientation and views.

South elevation

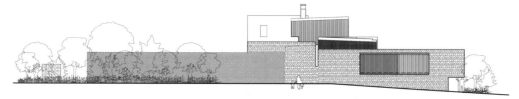

East elevation

First-floor plan

The layout is defined by stone blades
that bisect the house and delineate living
zones and pavilions.

## 002

Energy-efficient light bulbs use less energy than incandescent bulbs, which are highly inefficient. There are two types of energy-efficient light bulbs: compact fluorescent and light-emitting diodes

The house has been thermally engineered. In addition to green roofs, it features a number of sustainability initiatives, including 15 KW of solar power, skylights, and low-E glass throughout.

The use of reclaimed timber gives a space a sense of history. Most reclaimed timber is obtained from old barns and warehouses and is used in homes for siding and flooring.

**Big Little Rock**

Architects: Minarc
Location: Biskupstungur, Iceland
Photography: © Minarc

Big Little Rock is a modest house made to blend in with the surrounding landscape. Its simple eco-friendly design focuses on functionality and creates a healthy living environment for its occupants. While concrete, wood, and glass predominate and unify the construction style, conscious effort was made to use materials in their most natural form. The project also embraces history with shapes found in traditional mud houses.

## 004

A steel roof can contribute to the overall thermal efficiency of a home, lowering the costs of energy use and minimizing environmental impact.

## 005

Green roofs prevent thermal insulation from buoying up during heavy rainfall and protect it against UV radiation.

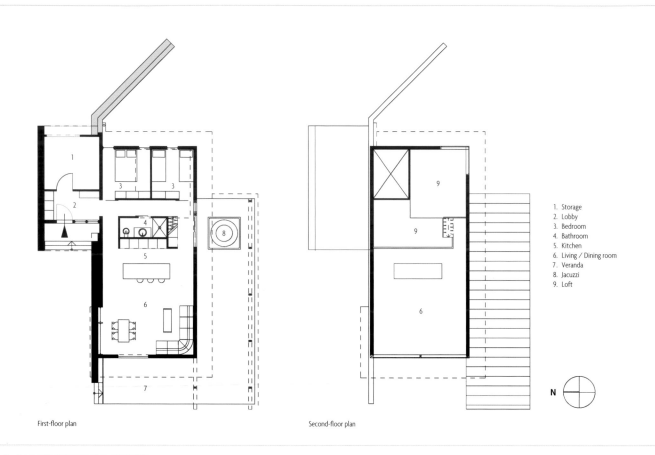

First-floor plan

Second-floor plan

1. Storage
2. Lobby
3. Bedroom
4. Bathroom
5. Kitchen
6. Living / Dining room
7. Veranda
8. Jacuzzi
9. Loft

N

# 006

Porches, carports, and breezeways can be created to take advantage of the unique environmental characteristics of a location.

## 007

In warm climates, sliding
doors are a good solution for
cooling a home, while offering
the possibility to spill indoor
activities outside.

## Villa L—Paradox of Uniting Diversity

Architects: Powerhouse
Company, RAU

Location: Utrecht,
the Netherlands

Photography: © Christian
van der Kooy

Villa L is a spatially diverse three-story construction, where every floor—one is partially buried in the ground—has its own identity. To respond to the desire for a functional division of space, the house has an open plan, oriented towards the sun and the views of the garden. The house incorporates innovative sustainable measures, including hot- and cold-water storage and extensive use of photovoltaic panels.

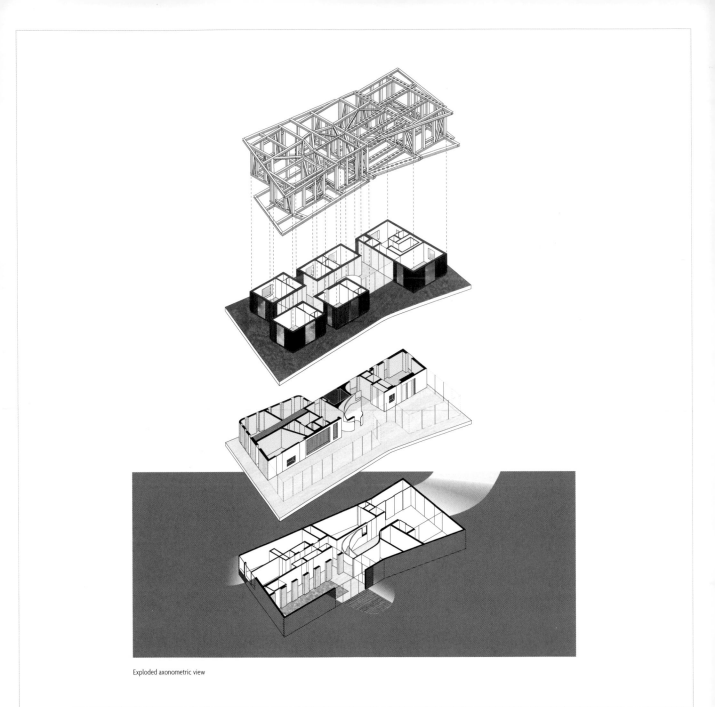

Exploded axonometric view

The second floor is a green plinth on top of which stand independent volumes accommodating various bedrooms. In that respect, every room is a world of its own, providing not only privacy, but also views.

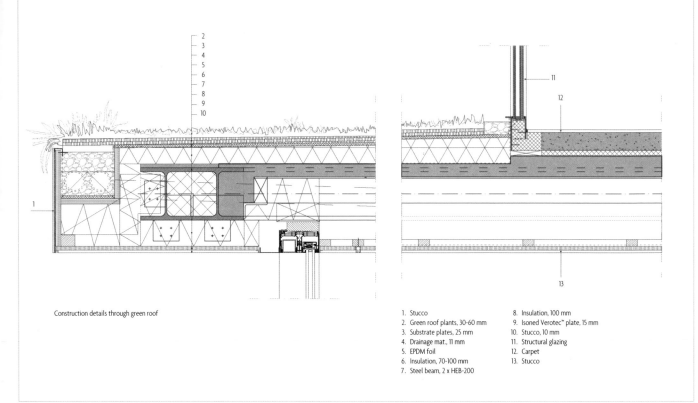

Construction details through green roof

1. Stucco
2. Green roof plants, 30-60 mm
3. Substrate plates, 25 mm
4. Drainage mat., 11 mm
5. EPDM foil
6. Insulation, 70-100 mm
7. Steel beam, 2 x HEB-200

8. Insulation, 100 mm
9. Isoned Verotec™ plate, 15 mm
10. Stucco, 10 mm
11. Structural glazing
12. Carpet
13. Stucco

## 008

The use of green roofs in construction offers benefits such as reducing heating and cooling costs, decreasing storm water run-off, and filtering pollutants and $CO_2$.

## 009

Different vegetation types with varying growth patterns can have different insulation properties affecting the level of heat transfer to and from the vegetation layer through the roofing system layers.

A small pavilion that can be used
as a guesthouse stands in a secluded
corner of the garden. Its mirrored glass
skin reflects the surroundings making
the structure almost invisible.

The excavations at the basement level allow the pool and guestrooms to have glazed façades and direct access to the garden. The basement also contains a dedicated area for high-end energy-saving systems.

## 010

A slim window frame optimizes day lighting and thermal performance. To minimize heat loss, a good solution is to inset the window frame behind the exterior insulation layer.

### Tarifa House

The site is located on a slope looking at the valley that dominates the Strait of Gibraltar. The design is guided by the particularities of the zone's climate and by the rules that dictate the vernacular architecture of Andalusian *pueblos blancos* (whitewashed hill towns) with patios and narrow streets. The goal was to create not simply a house but a complex that would promote outdoor activities as much as indoor ones.

Architects: James & Mau
Location: Tarifa, Spain
Photography: © Erika Mayer

The various modules are unified
by a large canopy, which provides
protection from solar radiation;
thus creating a microclimate.

## 011

Reduction of material costs, minimization of onsite waste, and reduction of construction time are advantages of modular home design.

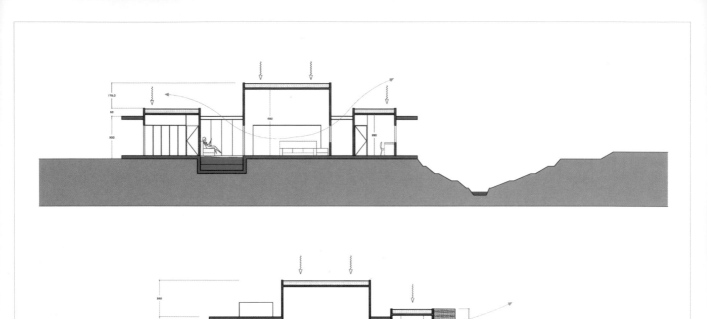

Sections

# 012

Modular construction is generally sturdier than its conventional counterpart because each module is engineered to withstand the rigors of transportation.

## 013

A breezeway is used to channel air between two structures, thereby producing a cooling effect. This effect can be reinforced with the presence of a shallow pool.

Sustainable materials and renewable energies like biomass and solar thermal energy are used for both heating rooms and heating water.

1. Entry hall
2. Coat room
3. Toilet
4. Terrace
5. Kitchen / Dining room
6. Bathroom
7. Bedroom
8. Living room
9. Reflecting pool
10. Terrace with permeable roofing
11. Swimming pool

Floor plan

## 014

Modular dwellings allow the separation of functions and promote a dynamic use of outdoor spaces.

## Yin-Yang House

Yin-Yang House is a net-zero energy single-family home for a growing family. Facing the street, the construction looks very enclosed; but once inside it shows that it is actually a series of courtyards that integrate with the interior of the house. The design is aimed to emphasize common spaces and promote interaction among family members.

Architects: Brooks + Scarpa
Location: Venice, CA, USA
Photography: © John Linden

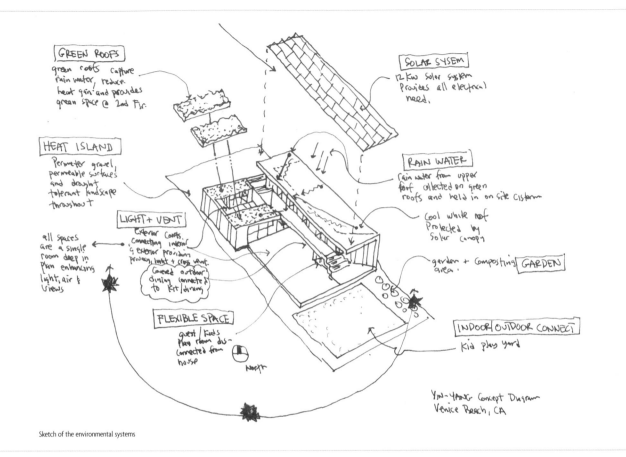

Sketch of the environmental systems

**GREEN ROOFS**
green roofs capture rain water, reduce heat gain and provides green space @ 2nd Flr.

**SOLAR SYSEM**
12 Kw solar system provies all electrical need.

**HEAT ISLAND**
Perimeter gravel, permeable surfaces and drought tolerant landscape throughout

**RAIN WATER**
rain water from upper roof collected on green roofs and held in on site cistern

Cool white roof Protected by Solar canopy

**LIGHT + VENT**
Exterior Courts. Connecting interior & exterior providion privacy, light + cross vent.
Covered outdoor dining connecto to kit/dining

all spaces are a single room deep in plan enhancing light, air & views

garden + composting area.   **GARDEN**

**FLEXIBLE SPACE**
guest/kids play room disconnected from house

North

**INDOOR OUTDOOR CONNECT**
Kid play yard

Yin-Yang Concept Diagram
Venice Beach, CA

# 015

When remodeling or building a house from scratch, consider the following principles of sustainable living: optimization of solar energy, improvement of indoor air quality, and use of high-performance materials.

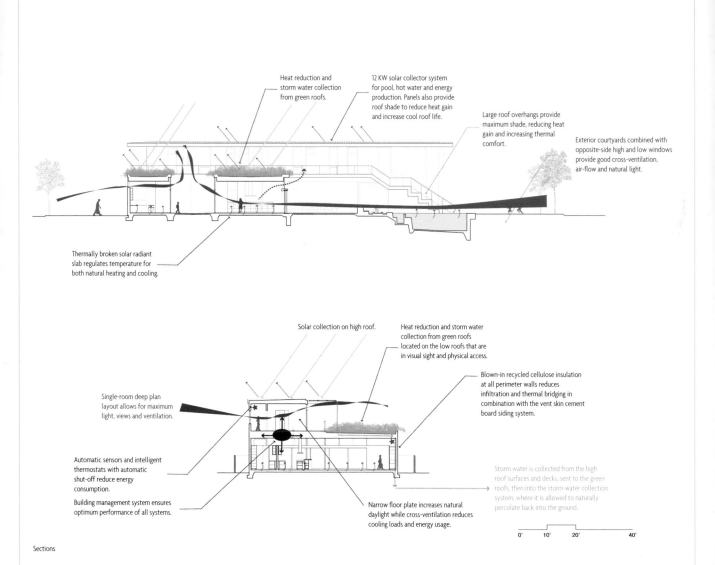

Heat reduction and storm water collection from green roofs.

12 KW solar collector system for pool, hot water and energy production. Panels also provide roof shade to reduce heat gain and increase cool roof life.

Large roof overhangs provide maximum shade, reducing heat gain and increasing thermal comfort.

Exterior courtyards combined with opposite-side high and low windows provide good cross-ventilation, air-flow and natural light.

Thermally broken solar radiant slab regulates temperature for both natural heating and cooling.

Solar collection on high roof.

Heat reduction and storm water collection from green roofs located on the low roofs that are in visual sight and physical access.

Blown-in recycled cellulose insulation at all perimeter walls reduces infiltration and thermal bridging in combination with the vent skin cement board siding system.

Single-room deep plan layout allows for maximum light, views and ventilation.

Automatic sensors and intelligent thermostats with automatic shut-off reduce energy consumption.

Building management system ensures optimum performance of all systems.

Narrow floor plate increases natural daylight while cross-ventilation reduces cooling loads and energy usage.

Storm water is collected from the high roof surfaces and decks, sent to the green roofs, then into the storm water collection system, where it is allowed to naturally percolate back into the ground.

0'    10'    20'              40'

Sections

The active systems in the home include a 12 KW solar photovoltaic panel system, which doubles as a sunshade device.

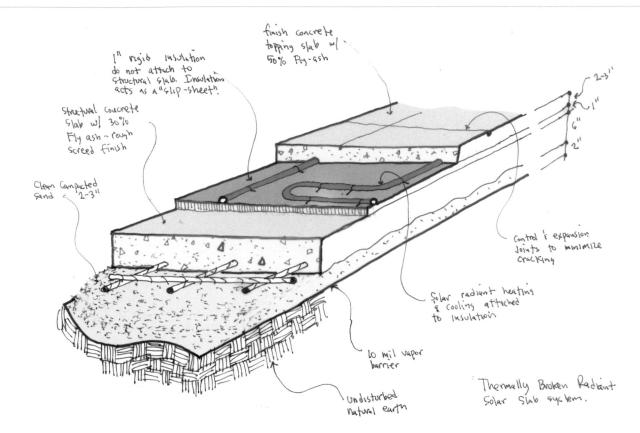

finish concrete topping slab w/ 50% Fly-ash

1" rigid insulation do not attach to Structural Slab. Insulation acts as a "slip-sheet".

Structural concrete Slab w/ 30% Fly ash - rough screed finish

Clean Compacted Sand ~ 2-3"

2-3"
1"
6"
2"

Control & expansion Joints to minimize cracking

Solar radiant heating & cooling attached to insulation

10 mil vapor barrier

Undisturbed natural earth

Thermally Broken Radiant Solar Slab system.

Detail sketch of radiant floor

016

Blown-in cellulose insulation and radiant floor heating contribute to an energy-efficient climate control system.

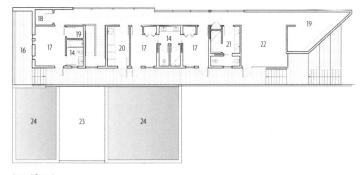

Second-floor plan

First-floor plan

| | | |
|---|---|---|
| 1. Entry | 10. Covered patio | 19. Closet |
| 2. Office | 11. Planter | 20. Laundry |
| 3. Garage | 12. Rec. room | 21. Master bathroom |
| 4. Mudroom | 13. Patio | 22. Master bedroom |
| 5. Courtyard | 14. Bathroom | 23. Open to below |
| 6. Pantry | 15. Shower | 24. Green roof |
| 7. Kitchen | 16. Front balcony | 25. Mechanical room |
| 8. Dining room | 17. Bedroom | 26. Pool |
| 9. Living room | 18. Storage | |

Eco-friendly materials like bamboo, composite stone, and recycled tile countertops and bathroom finishes are some of the house's environmental strategies.

## Stony Point House

**Architects:** Hays + Ewing Design Studio

**Location:** Stony Point, Charlottesville, VA, USA

**Photography:** © Prakash Patel

The owners of this home expressed interest in having a house that encouraged an appreciation of their three-acre wooded property and also served as a quiet space to support their contemplative, Zen-like lifestyle. The house and outdoor spaces are terraced into a hillside, taking advantage of the views. Unlike traditional, passive solar strategies, the length of the house is oriented exactly on solar north. The larger living spaces all open onto expansive terraces to the south and west.

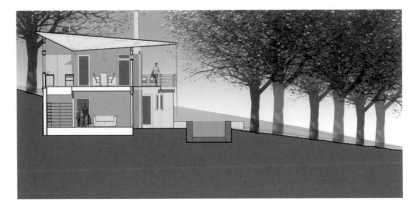

East-west section

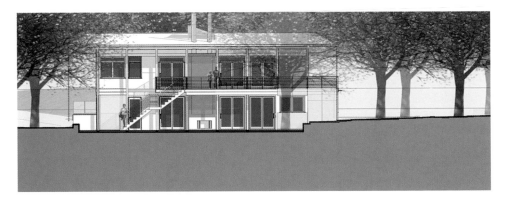

West elevation

The butterfly roof's deep overhang and tree canopy are to the west. They provide an optimal sunscreen in the summer and allow heat gain as needed in the winter.

Second-floor (entry) plan

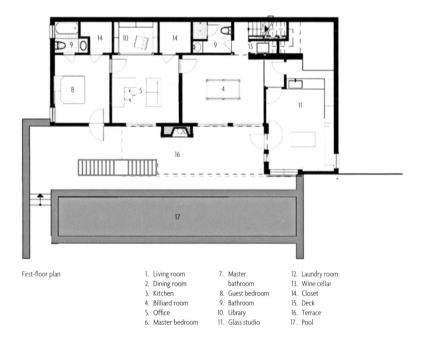

First-floor plan

1. Living room
2. Dining room
3. Kitchen
4. Billiard room
5. Office
6. Master bedroom
7. Master bathroom
8. Guest bedroom
9. Bathroom
10. Library
11. Glass studio
12. Laundry room
13. Wine cellar
14. Closet
15. Deck
16. Terrace
17. Pool

## 017

The evaporation of water has a cooling effect in hot and dry climates. A shallow pool in a breezeway is an effective cooling system, as the wind circulates through the breezeway and into the buildings on each side.

# 018

Open-plan spaces with openings on opposite walls provide natural breezes with a pathway through the room.

## 019

High clerestory windows on the eastern side of the house bring morning light into it. The inverted truss is steeply sloped to accentuate the lighting effect.

## Citriodora

Unadorned materials and simple, pragmatic detailing were used for the construction of the Citriodora house. The site rises moderately from the street, sheltered in the lee of a hill with two neighboring houses close by. A stand of lemon-scented gums occupies the northeast corner of the property, hence the name of the house. The climatic conditions, exposure, and building regulations provided both opportunities and constraints that informed the design material selection and detailing.

Architects: Seeley Architects
Location: Anglesea, Australia
Photography: © David Seeley,
Zoe Economides

The airborne salt spray and wind
required special design consideration.
As a result, the roof mimics the form
of the wind-pruned coastal vegetation.

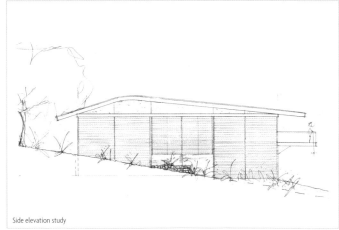

Side elevation study

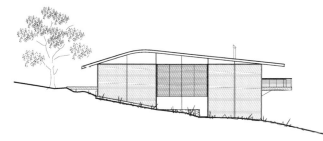

South elevation

East elevation

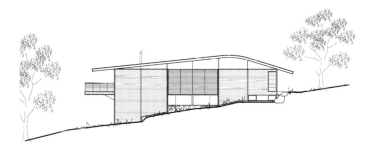

North elevation

West elevation

## 020

Climate should determine the shape of the roof and the materials used in its construction.

The shape of the house and the
materials used reference traditional
timber construction and archetypal
coastal homes.

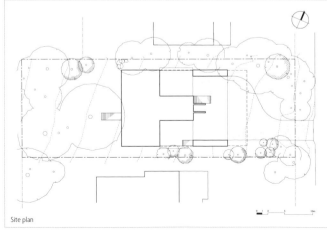

Site plan

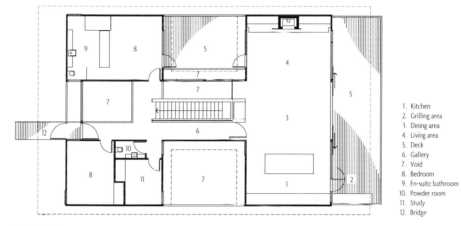

Second-floor plan

1. Kitchen
2. Grilling area
3. Dining area
4. Living area
5. Deck
6. Gallery
7. Void
8. Bedroom
9. En-suite bathroom
10. Powder room
11. Study
12. Bridge

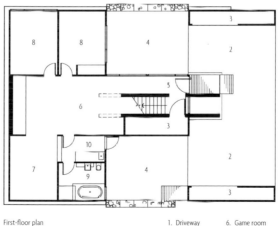

First-floor plan

1. Driveway
2. Carport
3. Storage
4. Courtyard
5. Entry
6. Game room
7. TV room
8. Bedroom
9. Bathroom
10. Laundry

0  1  2          5                    10m

## 021

Adding clerestories to a
kitchen can improve the level
and distribution of daylight,
creating a comfortable working
space. Because the light
comes from above eye level,
glare is not an issue.

## 022

Kitchen surfaces should be solid, non porous, and durable. Good sources are sustainably sourced or reclaimed wood or bamboo, stone, tiles, and concrete with recycled content.

The refined aesthetic of the interior is enhanced by slender steel and LVL (laminated veneer lumber) beams, deep overhangs, and large expanses of glass.

## 023

Consider using FSC (Forest
Stewardship Council) certified
wood ceiling panels in the
design of your home. Wood
panels provide a Class A
fire rating and resistance
to humidity.

### Ingoldsby House

The Ingoldsby House is a sensitive response to a coastal site requiring special consideration. The core idea for this house sprung from the piers that dot the coastal region of Victoria. The result is a building that utilizes a robust post and beam structure and explores the contrast between mass and void. The house is an extroverted form containing the living rooms and an introverted form containing bedrooms and bathrooms sitting over a partial basement.

Architects: Seeley Architects
Location: Anglesea, Australia
Photography: © Shannon
McGrath

The use of recycled timbers
and long-lasting materials,
the minimal destruction of
vegetation, and the use of
water storage tanks mitigate the
impact of this new construction
on the environment.

Angling the louvers up allows
natural light into the house.
Angling the louvers down
helps bring the cool air in
without letting in much light
or giving up privacy.

## 026

High lighting and ventilation levels can be achieved through breezeways and louvered clerestories.

The materials were chosen for their durability and low maintenance requirements. They help minimize the solid waste problems and contribute to the energy-efficient nature of the house.

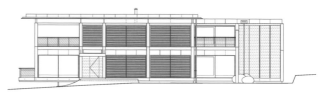

North elevation

East elevation

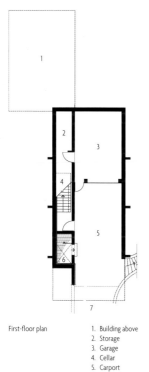

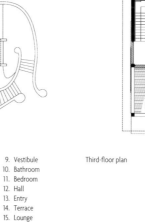

First-floor plan

1. Building above
2. Storage
3. Garage
4. Cellar
5. Carport
6. Shower
7. Driveway

Second-floor plan

1. Bedroom
2. Toilet
3. Bathroom
4. Hall
5. Bedroom
6. Deck
7. Bedroom
8. Laundry
9. Vestibule
10. Bathroom
11. Bedroom
12. Hall
13. Entry
14. Terrace
15. Lounge

Third-floor plan

1. Study
2. Toilet
3. En-suite bathroom
4. Deck
5. Hall
6. Bedroom
7. Dining room
8. Kitchen
9. Living room

N

The design of the house promotes
the notion of a coastal experience with
a sturdy structure, weathered materials,
and a connection between enclosed
and open spaces.

The Essex House project is a 500 sq. ft. addition to an existing 970 sq. ft. weatherboard house that sits at one end of a long and narrow plot. The addition has an elongated plan and extends along the southern side of the backyard. Walls are kept to a minimum with fully glazed garage-style doors that open the rooms to the outdoor space and wood slat screens that filter light. Sustainability is intrinsic to this design.

## Essex Street House

Architects: Andrew Maynard Architects

Location: Brunswick, Melbourne, Australia

Photography: © Andrew Maynard Architects, Peter Bennetts

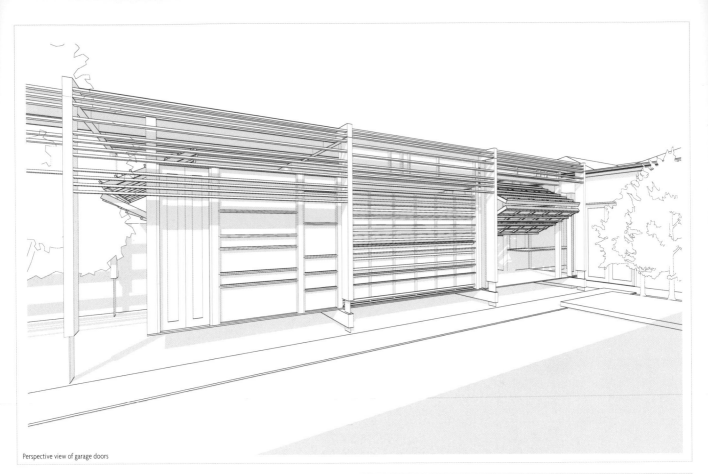

Perspective view of garage doors

## 027

The use of exposed structures that minimize the need for finishes and a building's carbon footprint analysis are two considerations of sustainable design that are gaining strength in residential architecture.

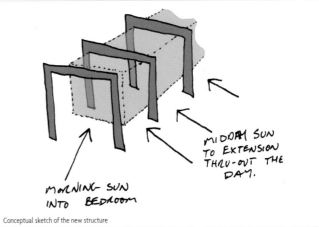

MORNING SUN INTO BEDROOM

MIDDAY SUN TO EXTENSION THRU-OUT THE DAY.

Conceptual sketch of the new structure

Interior-perspective rendering

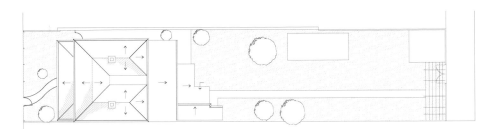

Existing roof plan

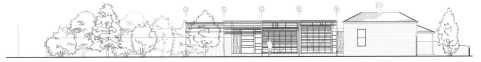

Proposed north elevation

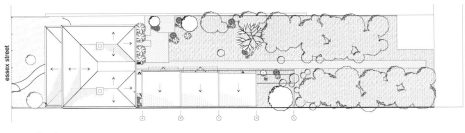

essex street

Proposed floor plan

# 028

A structure that is lifted off the ground allows for the landscape to regenerate after construction is completed and also, if need be, facilitates the removal of the building.

## 029

Swing-up-and-fold garage doors maximize solar exposure and allow interior activities to spill outdoors.

RECYCLED
IRON BARK

RECYCLED &
FARMED
TIMBERS
USED TO
MINIMISE
ENVIRONMENTAL
IMPACT.

ENVIRONMENT

Corner detail of recycled gray iron bark portal frame

The design of this house integrates rustic materials and harnesses natural forces to bring exterior materials to the interior. Local building traditions and the availability of materials in the immediate vicinity yielded a wealth of ideas and inspiration. A thorough assessment of the sun path, views, and landscape features determined the best strategies to meet climate-appropriate comfort and sustainability requirements.

## Outside IN House

Architect: Fernanda Vuillemier
Location: Puerto Natales, Chile
Photography: © Daniel Bruhin

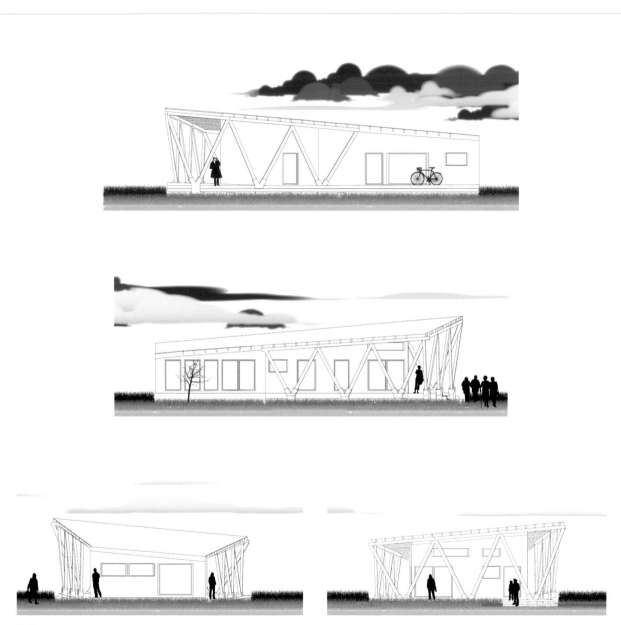

Elevations

## 030

A sloping roof directs
the prevailing wind in one
direction, and also facilitates
the collection of rainwater.

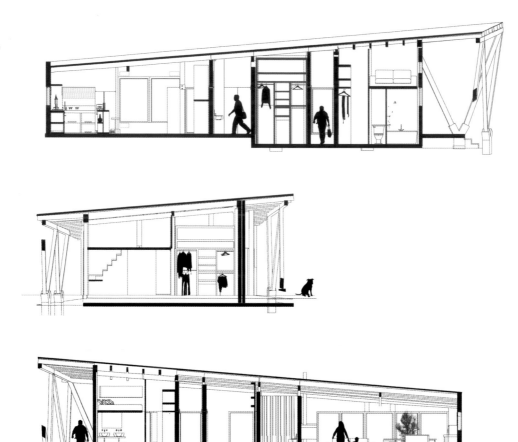

Sections

The house is equipped with passive solar features to absorb, store, and distribute solar resources for heating, cooling, and lighting.

## 031

Raise the floor from the ground and insulate it properly to prevent it from absorbing moisture. Insulation is required to minimize heat loss through the ground.

## 032

The renewable and recyclable nature of wood and its minimal embodied energy make timber a good exterior wall cladding material.

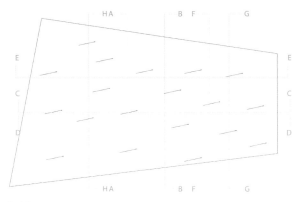

Roof plan

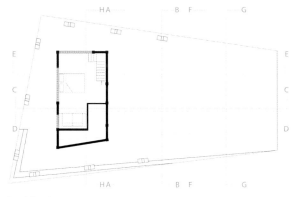

Second-floor plan

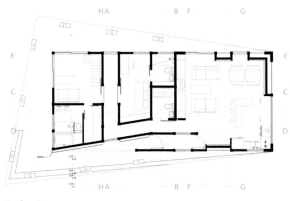

First-floor plan

Functions that could be done outdoors were evaluated to determine how much the building could expand during the summer and shrink in the winter.

## Villa Rieteiland-Oost

Villa Rieteiland-Oost is a mix-use building that stands out for its size and all-wood skin. Its timber structure is clad in sustainably sourced cedar slats laid horizontally and vertically, with similarly covered shutters to camouflage the openings and make the overall appearance of the building more homogeneous. A spiral staircase tucked into a recess in the front façade leads directly to an office on the third floor.

Architects: Fgeon Architecten

Location: Amsterdam, the Netherlands

Photography: © Chiel de Nooyer

An active façade adapts to the needs of the homeowners and the effects of the seasons. Shutters can either be open to let light and warmth into the house or closed to screen the sunlight out and keep the interior cool.

top f bor

Perspective view

## 033

Reclaimed wood is an eco friendly material worth considering when building or renovating a home. One of wood's qualities to note is that it stores carbon; it doesn't release it into the atmosphere.

## 034

A common characteristic of
passive solar homes involves
thermal mass in the floor
beneath the south-facing
windows, as it retains
sun-produced heat.

## 035

To optimize the advantages of a sustainable home, attention should be paid to details such as thermal bridging, high insulation values of the roof, and wall and floor assemblies.

## 036

Reclaimed wood makes construction more affordable. Not only is wood environmentally friendly, but it also enhances the aesthetic value of a home.

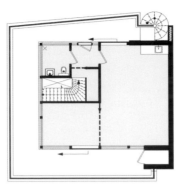

Third-floor plan

Second-floor plan

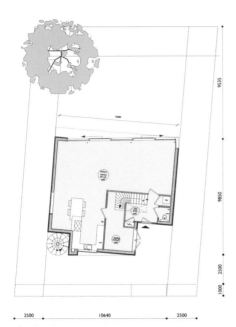

9535

9850

2500

1000

2500          10640          2500

Site plan

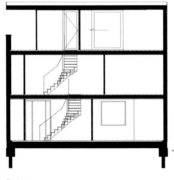

Section

First-floor plan

## 037

Windows' sizes and proportions can vary depending on how well insulated a house is and how energy efficient its glazing is.

When untreated, wood is completely
biodegradable at the end of its useful life.

## 038

In cool climates, the thermal mass of concrete can absorb solar gain. This allows the minimization of the need for non-renewable heating energy.

### Modernist Summer Hamptons Residence

As this house is used primarily in the summer, its main gathering spaces are outdoors. The large glass panels slide into the exterior walls so that the house can have a large porch. The solid volumes feature Port Oxford cedar used in two different exterior details: as solid siding and as horizontal slats. Aesthetically, this design decision achieves visual interest and functionally, and accommodates different levels of privacy.

Architects: Austin Patterson Disston Architects

Location: Quogue, NY, USA

Photography: © Peter Murdock

North elevation

East elevation

South elevation

West elevation

The exterior walls of the house combine two cladding methods: horizontal tongue-and-groove siding and wooden-slat screening. Both provide different levels of privacy, while enriching the visual texture of the building.

The two wings of the building embrace a courtyard. The interlocking volumes of the house and the L-shape swimming pool establish a relationship between solid and void, and interior and exterior.

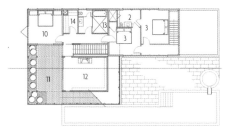

Second-floor plan

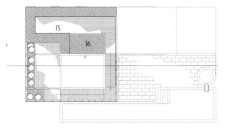

Roof plan

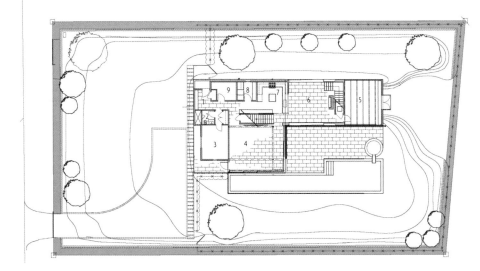

First-floor plan

1. Mud room
2. Bathroom
3. Bedroom
4. Living room
5. Studio
6. Family and dining room
7. Kitchen
8. Laundry
9. Mechanical room
10. Master bedroom
11. Deck / Garden
12. Library
13. Master bathroom
14. Master closet
15. Roof deck
16. Roof garden

## 039

Wooden screens can complement the look of your house while providing solutions to privacy and security concerns.

## 040

Environmentally certified and
reclaimed wood is available in
standard dimensional lumber.
Using certified framing lumber,
plywood, and reclaimed beams
can save money.

The house has ground-source heat pumps and a highly insulated envelope with solar voltaic and solar hot water. It also incorporates LED and low-voltage lighting.

**Harpoon House**

Architects: Design for
Occupancy
Location: Portland, OR, USA
Photography: © Matt Kirkpatrick

Located on an urban infill lot, Harpoon House occupies a small footprint—rather than taking up the total area allowed for its construction—in order to have a generous outdoor space. The three-story home was built with sustainability as an organizing principle. By integrating the design of interior spaces with habitable eco-roofs, decks, and patios, Harpoon House was designed to encourage a fluid relationship between indoor and outdoor living.

South elevation

West elevation

A ventilated wooden rainscreen made of untreated cedar slats is held off the concrete structure of the building. It serves as siding and as a screen where openings in the concrete structure occur.

## 041

Utility pipes can be concealed in the space between a rainscreen and an exterior wall. This eliminates the need to carve out panel insulation, which would result in thermal bridging.

# 042

A rainscreen is the weather-facing surface of an exterior wall used to minimize the forces driving moisture into the wall and manage energy transfer.

Second-floor plan

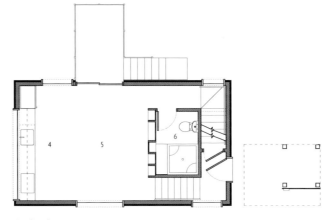

First-floor plan

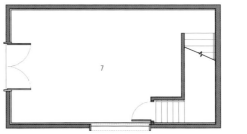

Basement-floor plan

1. Bedroom
2. Roof garden
3. Eco roof
4. Kitchen
5. Living room
6. Bathroom
7. Storage and cellar

## 043

Take advantage of a protected rooftop to grow your own vegetable and herb garden. Use containers and raised beds to avoid damage to the waterproofing membrane.

## 044

A rainscreen provides
additional protection from
the elements. It can also
double as a screen to shelter
an outdoor space such as
a balcony or a roof terrace.

### Peel House

This addition to an existing house provides a distinct visual separation of the two, while still unraveling its exterior surfaces to embrace the existing structure. The exterior surfaces of the building are made up of stacked cedar pieces that are assembled at surface intersections. The detailing of this allows for opaque areas and for partially transparent areas along the building's exterior.

Architects: **Taylor & Miller**

Location: **The Berkshires, MA, USA**

Photography: © **Taylor & Miller, Gregory Sherin**

Partially transparent areas allow for sunshade, privacy, ventilation, and a connection to the natural environment.

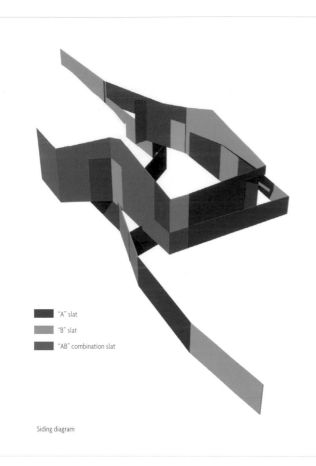

"A" slat

"B" slat

"AB" combination slat

Siding diagram

# 045

There is no need for the use of various materials to make the skin of a building visually interesting. Wood is a versatile material that lends itself to any shape, size, and construction method.

# 046

Woodworking joinery techniques highlight the beauty of wood. Reclaimed timber already has character of its own.

## 047

The selection of wood for siding can depend on the availability of resources; but cedar, fir, and redwood provide material for a sturdy siding resistant to the elements.

The wooden exterior of the building will weather into silvery gray tones, and it will slowly blend with the surrounding forest.

## 048

Before choosing the type of wood to use in a project, it is important to learn about the environmental benefits of FSC (Forest Stewardship Council) certified wood.

The interior of the house boasts the same level of attention to detail as the exterior with joinery details that create focal points.

## Pull House

A ranch home used to sit on this project. After the building was stripped down to its frame, the overall form was stretched longitudinally to house the necessary additional program. The house was built using sustainable materials and construction techniques such as reclaimed wood cladding for the exterior, bamboo for almost all interior surfaces, LED and fluorescent light fixtures, and low-VOC products.

Architects: Taylor & Miller
Location: The Berkshires, MA, USA
Photography: © Gregory Cherin

## 049

Wood-clad homes are durable as long as the wall assemblies include an adequate vapor layer and insulation to prevent rot and other moisture-related issues.

EXISTING HOUSE STRUCTURE

COMPLETELY NEW CONSTRUCTION

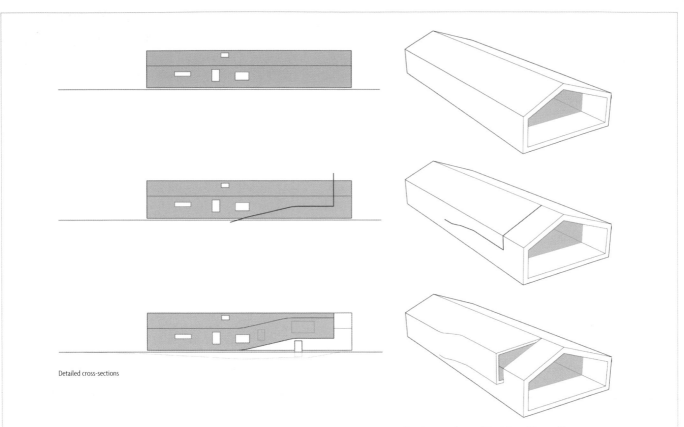

Detailed cross-sections

Extrusion process diagrams of the existing ranch home profile

The area defined by a volumetric slice is pulled up and out of the extruded boundaries, creating a semi-private loft space that hovers above the living and dining areas.

Punches of color highlight the openings along the exterior wall of the protrusion. More than a simple design statement, these colors reveal the volume of the walls, which house thick insulation.

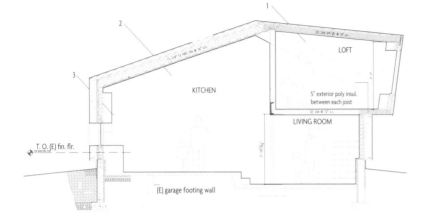

LOFT

KITCHEN

LIVING ROOM

5" exterior poly insul. between each joist.

T. O. (E) fin. flr.

(E) garage footing wall

1. NEW ROOF ASSEMBLY
   Cedar roofing over 1 x 4 sleepers over rubber membrane roofing over 5/8" CDX plywood over (2) 2 x 8 SPF rafters @ 16" O.C. with 7" extruded polystyrene insulation between each rafter under ¾" wood paneling

2. NEW ROOF ASSEMBLY
   Cedar roofing over 2 x 4 sleepers over rubber membrane roofing over 5/8" CDX plywood over 11-7/8" TJI PRO 150 rafters @ 16" O.C. with Prop-R-Vent and (2) layers R-19 BATT insulation between each rafter with 1" rigid expanded polystyrene insulation over underside of rafters; tape joints under ½" painted gypboard; provide continuous vent @ ridge and eave

3. TYPICAL NEW WALL ASSEMBLY
   Cedar siding over 2 x 6 sleepers over rubber membrane roofing over 2" extruded polystyrene rigid insulation over ¾" furring over ½" CDX plywood over 2 x 6 studs @ 16" O.C. with R-19 BATT insulation between each stud under 3 mil. Poly vapor barrier under painted gypboard

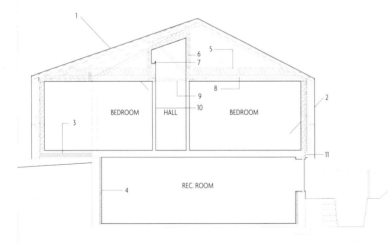

BEDROOM
HALL
BEDROOM
REC. ROOM

Detailed cross-sections

1. EXISTING ROOF ASSEMBLY
   Cedar roofing over 2 x 4 sleepers over rubber membrane roofing over 5/8" CDX plywood over tapered furring over existing roof with R-38 BATT insulation over existing loose fill insulation under ½" painted gypboard; provide continuous vent @ ridge and eave

2. EXISTING WALL ASSEMBLY
   Cedar siding over 2 x 6 sleepers over rubber membrane roofing over 2" extruded polystyrene rigid insulation over ¾" furring over existing horizontal siding over ½" plywood over 2 x 6 studs @ 16" O.C. with R-19 BATT insulation between each stud under existing wood paneling under 3 mil. Poly vapor barrier under painted gypboard

3. 5" exterior poly insulation between each joist

4. New 2" polystyrene insulation over existing concrete foundation walls under ¾" furring under ½" painted gypboard.

5. New R-38 BATTS

6. R-21 @ walls above ceiling

7. Lighting trough

8. Existing loose fill insulation

9. Install new ½" steel rod cross-tie before cutting existing ceiling joist to raise hallway ceiling

10. New non-load-bearing partition walls

11. Bolt C9 x 20 A36 to existing rim with (2) 1-1/ 2" x 2" galvanized bolts @ 16" O.C. before cutting foundation wall for new basement access.

In contrast with the silvery finish of the white cedar exterior cladding, colorful touches at the window and door openings give a hint of the vibrant interior.

## 050

Bamboo is a renewable, sustainable resource. It is a low-resin, open-grain material that takes stains and finishes well. These qualities make bamboo a suitable material for interior applications.

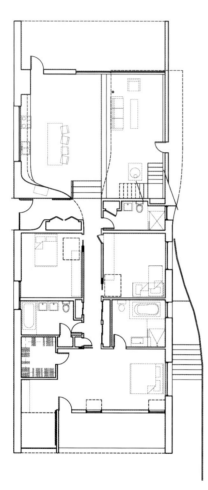

Main-floor plan

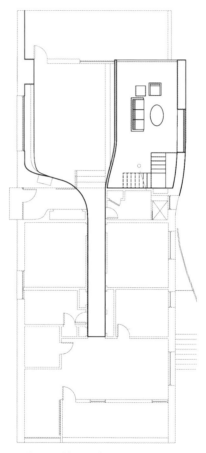

Upper "semi-private" living room floor plan

Two bamboo-clad walls organize the interior layout. They run parallel to each other forming a narrow passage that gives access to the bedrooms, and then funnel out to give room to an ample living space.

## Villa Nyberg

This house has a circular plan with a central courtyard that allows occupants to enjoy daylight from different directions. Villa Nyberg is a well-insulated building that is largely heated by the energy generated from body heat and household equipment. The round shape of the house eliminates cold bridges and minimizes the enclosing wall area of the house, reducing heat loss.

Architects: Kjellgren Kaminsky Architecture

Location: Borlänge, Sweden

Photography: © Kjellgren Kaminsky Architecture

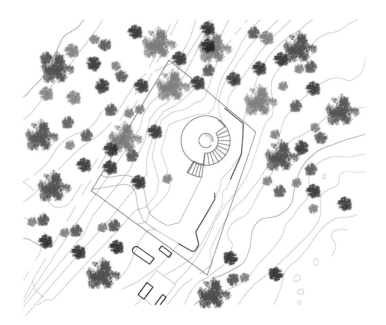

Site plan

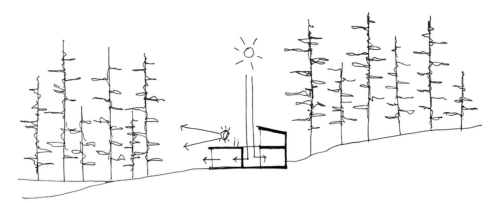

Sketch of sunlight optimization

Untreated-pine wood siding was used to facilitate the integration of the construction into the landscape. With time the wood will weather and turn gray, like the tree trunks of the surrounding forest.

TIME...

TRANSLATED INTO HOW WE LIVE...

Take a shower
Leisure
Eat
Sleep
Eat / Shower
Work

CAN GET A HOUSE

Clock diagram

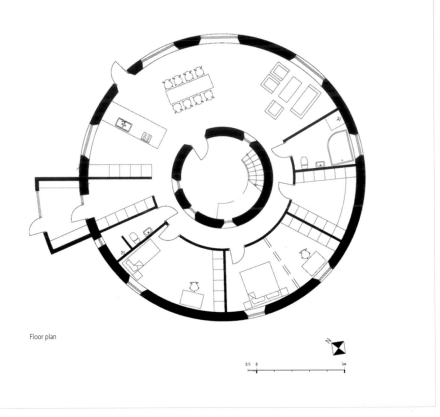

Floor plan

N

0.5  0                                    5m

# 051

People and home equipment generate energy that contributes to the passive heating system of a well-insulated home.

## 052

Exterior wall systems can wrap a building with a thermal protection layer that prevents energy loss through thermal bridges.

### 3716 Springfield

Architects: Studio 804
Location: Kansas City, KS, USA
Photography: © Studio 804

This project is an environmentally conscious modern home, which performs completely off the grid. As the first LEED platinum home in the Kansas City metropolitan area, the building serves as an example of sustainable living for people who want to live close to an urban center. The house features a combination of passive and active systems.

Second-floor plan

1. Bedroom
2. Stair core
3. Bathroom
4. Bathroom
5. Bedroom
6. Porch

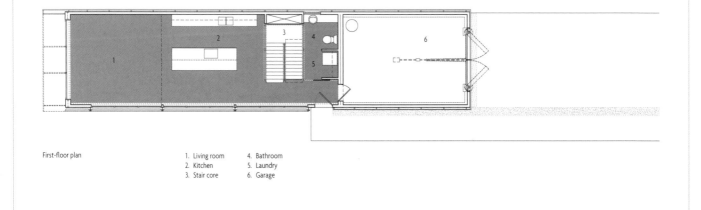

First-floor plan

1. Living room
2. Kitchen
3. Stair core
4. Bathroom
5. Laundry
6. Garage

Wood was the natural choice for this
building due to its economic value, ease
of assembly, and speed of construction.
FSC-certified wood was used in the
framing and sheathing of all walls,
the roof, and the floor.

A rainscreen made of the FSC-certified tropical wood Cumaru wraps the entire house. It compartmentalizes the air cavity, thereby allowing rapid air-pressure equalization and minimal moisture intrusion.

## 053

Landscape features such as trees, rock formations, water, and wind patterns can influence how a house performs. This knowledge will help you set the foundation for an energy-efficient home.

All countertops and bathroom surrounds are manufactured from a recycled paper composite material that is highly durable, low maintenance, and stain resistant.

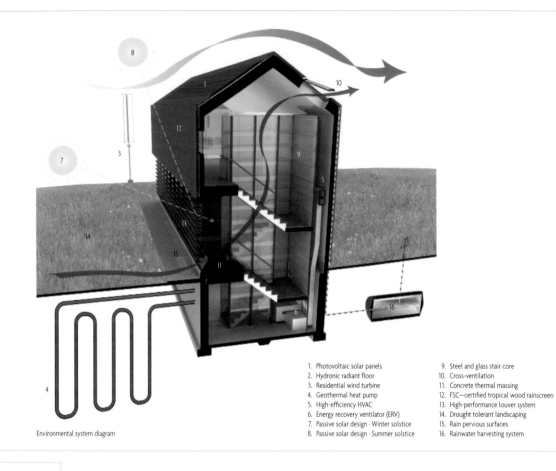

1. Photovoltaic solar panels
2. Hydronic radiant floor
3. Residential wind turbine
4. Geothermal heat pump
5. High-efficiency HVAC
6. Energy recovery ventilator (ERV)
7. Passive solar design · Winter solstice
8. Passive solar design · Summer solstice
9. Steel and glass stair core
10. Cross-ventilation
11. Concrete thermal massing
12. FSC—certified tropical wood rainscreen
13. High-performance louver system
14. Drought tolerant landscaping
15. Rain pervious surfaces
16. Rainwater harvesting system

Environmental system diagram

## 054

The use of renewable energy from the sun, wind, and thermal energy stored in the earth's crust can allow a home to rely less on non-renewable sources such as fossil fuels, coal, and natural gas.

FSC-certified Jatoba hardwood flooring is featured in the upstairs loft and bedroom spaces and continues to wrap the kitchen ceiling to achieve a visual link between spaces.

### Prescott Passive House

Architects: Studio 804
Location: Kansas City, KS, USA
Photography: © Studio 804

This low-energy house is designed for the affordable-housing market. Its exterior is clad in a charred Douglas fir rainscreen with louvers that are angled to allow winter heat gain and block sunlight from penetrating the house in the summer. Designed to exceed both Passivehaus and LEED platinum standards, the residence uses low-cost passive strategies such as thermal mass, high-performance windows, high insulation, southern orientation, and an airtight building envelope.

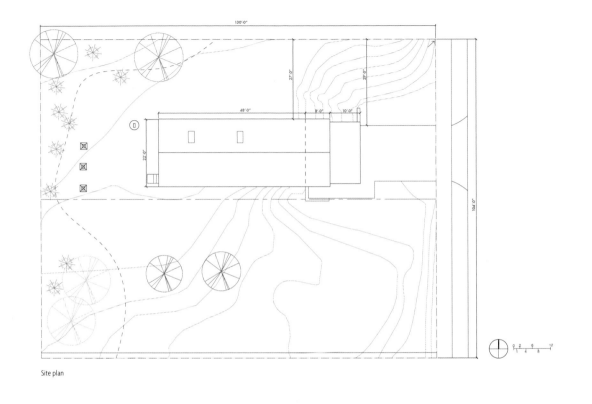

Site plan

# 055

An airtight building exterior
can avoid a heat transfer
between the interior and the
exterior. This allows a home
to retain the heat of an interior
high-performance glazing.

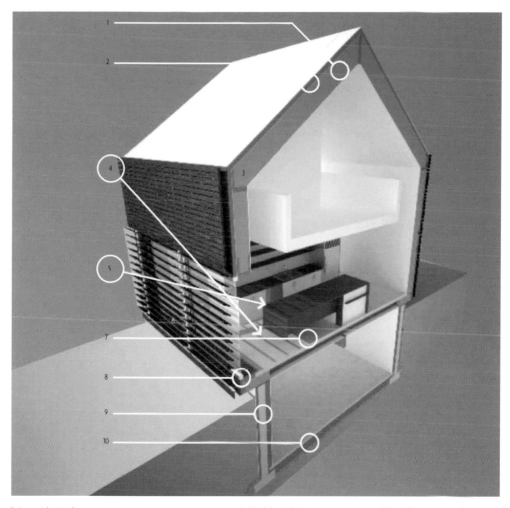

Environmental system diagram

1. 16" cellulose insulation
2. 3" extruded polystyrene (XPS)
3. The deep cavities provided by the engineered lumber framing allow for a super-insulated blanket to surround the house
4. Passive solar design. Summer solstice
5. Passive solar design. Winter solstice
6. External louvers are oriented at an optimal angle to block summer sun and allow the winter sun deep into the space
7. 4" concrete slab
8. Triple-pane insulated frame windows
9. ICF foundation walls with additional XPS insulation
10. 4" concrete slab above 6" XPS insulation

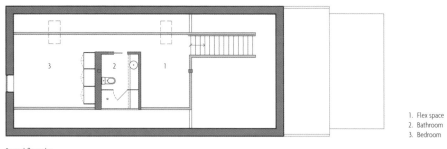

Second-floor plan

1. Flex space
2. Bathroom
3. Bedroom

First-floor plan

1. Flex space
2. Bedroom
3. Bathroom
4. Kitchen
5. Living room
6. Porch

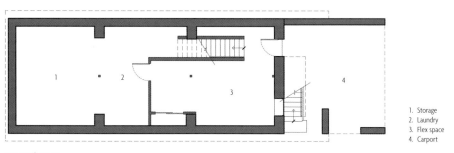

Basement-floor plan

1. Storage
2. Laundry
3. Flex space
4. Carport

A concrete floor can absorb and store heat for longer periods of time than other commonly used materials such as wood. This is due to its high density, which can also smooth out temperature variations.

Skylights reduce the need for air-conditioning in the summer and provide solar heat in the winter. An alternative to conventional skylights is solar tubes, which use light-intensifying devices to direct light.

Window size and orientation are design elements that can reduce the use of heating and cooling energy. Glazing technologies can provide insulating and solar protection.

**MODERNest House 1**

MODERNest is a new design and development initiative with a mission to offer affordable, sustainable, architect-designed houses in downtown Toronto neighborhoods. MODERNest sites are selected to provide easy access to good schools, public parks, transit lines, and local shops. House 1 is integrated with nearby houses through its scale and use of natural materials.

Architects: Kyra Clarkson, Christopher Glaisek/ MODERNest

Location: Toronto, ON, Canada

Photography: © Steven Evans

High-efficiency mechanical systems, low-E glass, and well-insulated walls combine to make House 1 a home with a modern spirit aspiring to revitalize the urban neighborhood.

## 059

An open-riser staircase makes a good light and airshaft. When combined with carefully placed operable windows it provides efficient ventilation and good overhead lighting.

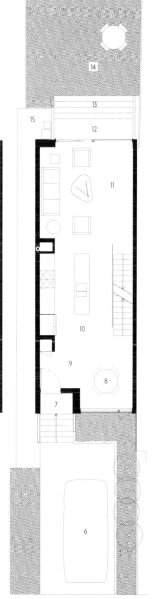

Basement-floor plan

Second-floor plan

First-floor plan

1. Bathroom and laundry
2. Furnace room
3. Built-in storage
4. Play area
5. Family room
6. One-car parking pad
7. Covered entry
8. Dining room
9. Foyer
10. Kitchen
11. Living room
12. Rear deck
13. Steps to garden
14. Landscaped garden
15. Waste bins
16. Second bedroom
17. Third bedroom
18. En-suite bathroom
19. Master bedroom

# 060

Windows placed higher than eighty-three inches from the floor are called daylight panels. The closer a daylight panel is to the ceiling, the more efficient it is in bringing light into a space.

Locally made Douglas fir windows
and sliding glass doors provide natural
ventilation and a strong connection
to the exterior landscape.

### Gabion House

The creation of this house embraced passive design, regional materials, and a local labor force. It also relied on sensible materials, defined as ones that embrace different textures and reinterpret their usage for the integration of indoor and outdoor spaces to maximize the usage of the space. The key characteristic of this home and the reason for its name is its rock walls, the "gabions," which integrate the house into its arid environment while protecting it from the sun and wind.

Architects: ColectivoMX
Location: San José del Cabo, Mexico
Photography: © Lifestyle & Editorial Photography

## 061

Gabion baskets have been traditionally used as retaining walls and as an erosion control solution. Today using gabions is a popular form of wall construction and provides ventilation and drainage.

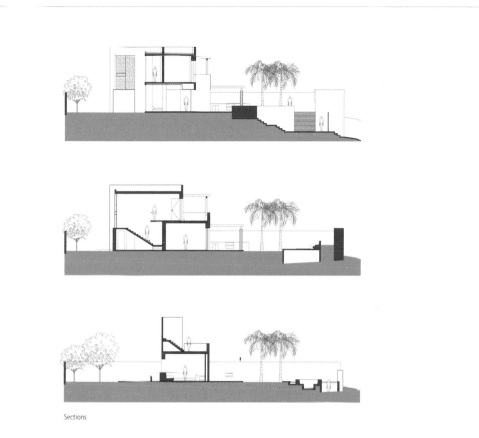

Sections

The house is surrounded by a canopy-shaded deck, which allows for comfortable outdoor living.

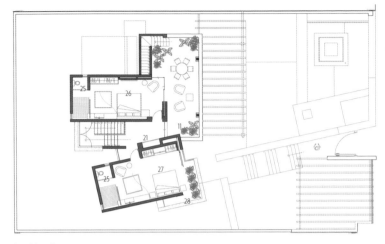

Second-floor plan

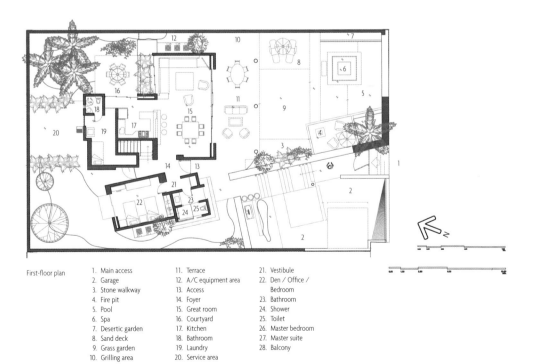

First-floor plan

| | | | |
|---|---|---|---|
| 1. Main access | 11. Terrace | 21. Vestibule |
| 2. Garage | 12. A/C equipment area | 22. Den / Office / |
| 3. Stone walkway | 13. Access | Bedroom |
| 4. Fire pit | 14. Foyer | 23. Bathroom |
| 5. Pool | 15. Great room | 24. Shower |
| 6. Spa | 16. Courtyard | 25. Toilet |
| 7. Desertic garden | 17. Kitchen | 26. Master bedroom |
| 8. Sand deck | 18. Bathroom | 27. Master suite |
| 9. Grass garden | 19. Laundry | 28. Balcony |
| 10. Grilling area | 20. Service area | |

Some walls are formed by a metal gabion-type framework filled with volcanic rock. Their purpose is to shield the house from the intense sun and heat, while allowing air to move through the space.

062

To minimize the use of
non-renewable resources,
try to rely on the possibilities
of natural materials.

## 063

LED lights have a considerably lower environmental impact than compact fluorescent lamps and an even lower impact than incandescent lighting over the lifetime of the products.

Architects: ÁBATON Architects
Location: Cáceres, Spain
Photography: © ÁBATON,
Belén Imaz

The ruins of an abandoned stable were the starting point of an extensive remodeling project that resulted in a self-sufficient family home. Far from any water supply and electrical grid, this stone building is located below two streams that flow all year round. They provide water for domestic use and hydroelectricity. The orientation of the house allows for sunlight to be the main source of heating during the cold months.

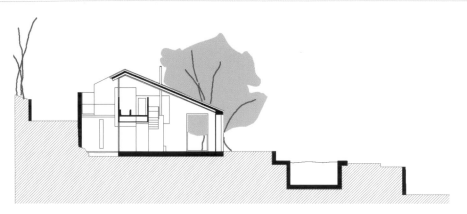

Cross-section

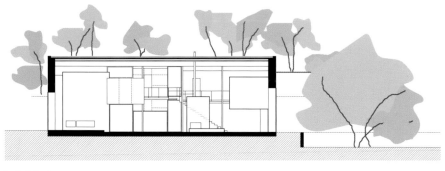

Longitudinal section

064

Sloping sites can present
the opportunity for innovative
house designs with minimal
excavation work, which would
detract from the topography's
character.

The crumbling stone walls and damaged timber structure were mostly replaced. Exposed concrete, steel beams, and limestone floors were built.

Patios and interior courtyards can be
used as outdoor rooms. These spaces
can be most effectively used when
protected from wind and excessive sun
exposure by tall walls and tree canopies.

## 065

Air circulation, evaporative
cooling, and the earth's
thermal mass are fundamental
passive cooling methods
for optimizing comfort.

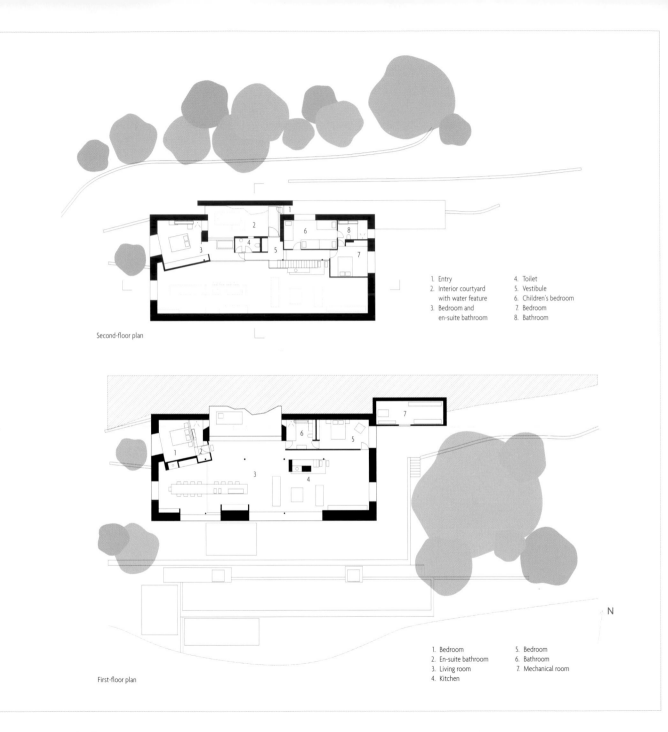

Second-floor plan

1. Entry
2. Interior courtyard with water feature
3. Bedroom and en-suite bathroom
4. Toilet
5. Vestibule
6. Children's bedroom
7. Bedroom
8. Bathroom

First-floor plan

1. Bedroom
2. En-suite bathroom
3. Living room
4. Kitchen
5. Bedroom
6. Bathroom
7. Mechanical room

N

## 066

Consider orienting a home
so that the side with most
openings is exposed to
breezes, and the opposite side,
with fewer openings, draws
these breezes through and out.

## 067

Concrete floors and masonry
walls provide thermal
mass. Their performance
is most efficient when
exposed to winter sun and
summer breezes.

## 068

The use of natural, local materials such as stone can add to the sustainable nature of a home. Stone requires little processing and if locally sourced requires little transporting.

Green Orchard is a new 200 square meter carbon neutral house set within 2,675 square meter of landscaped gardens. The house replaces a dilapidated single-story dwelling with a contemporary low-rise four-bedroom home. Both the house and landscape were designed with a specific intent to reduce consumption and the requirement for energy. All living spaces are open-plan to give a greater sense of openness and to maximize views and sunlight.

Architects: **Paul Archer Design**
Location: Compton Greenfield, United Kingdom
Photography: © Will Pryce

## 069

Using building elements prefabricated in a workshop can minimize the production of construction waste.

green orchard

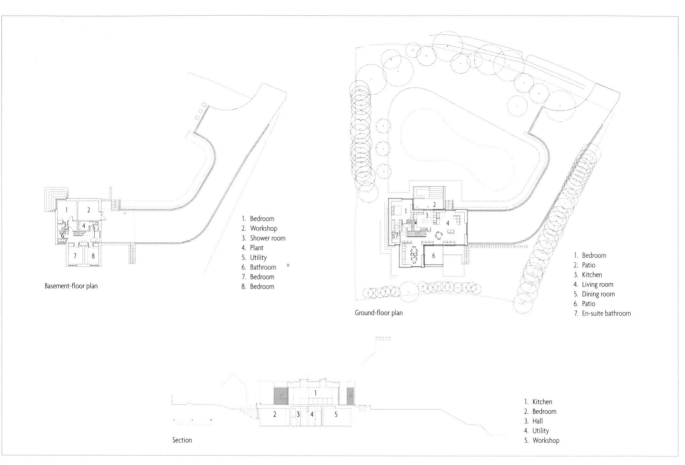

Basement-floor plan

1. Bedroom
2. Workshop
3. Shower room
4. Plant
5. Utility
6. Bathroom
7. Bedroom
8. Bedroom

Ground-floor plan

1. Bedroom
2. Patio
3. Kitchen
4. Living room
5. Dining room
6. Patio
7. En-suite bathroom

Section

1. Kitchen
2. Bedroom
3. Hall
4. Utility
5. Workshop

070

A green roof integrates
architecture into the landscape.
It also filters out pollutants
and acts as an active insulator.

The skin of the building is made of bespoke highly insulated panels, which are electronically motorized to slide open. They allow the occupants to control and vary the thermal performance of the house.

A wood-burning stove is the only heat source for the inhabitants. Thermal solar panels yield heating for 80 percent of the house's water. Photovoltaic panels provide electricity.

## 071

The use of skylights can translate into significant energy savings. A home with a good spread of natural light will benefit from passive solar gain and a reduced requirement for artificial lighting.

## Alan-Voo House

The clients for this house renovation asked that the area of their existing 1,000 sq. ft. house be doubled. It was determined that an extension could be attached to the existing structure. The addition has sculptural qualities and reflects the artistic personalities of the clients. It features a futuristic envelope with large expanses of glass and angular surfaces. The construction is proof that a high-tech look and sustainability can coexist.

Architects: Neil M. Denari Architects

Location: Los Angeles, CA, USA

Photography: © Benny Chan

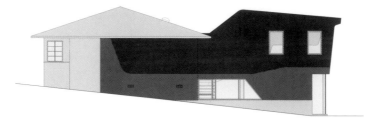

South elevation

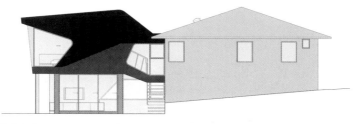

North elevation

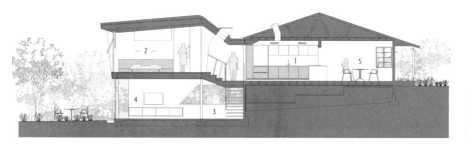

Section

1. Kitchen
2. Bedroom
3. Hall
4. Living room
5. Dining room

## 072

The less partitions dividing
a space, the more opportunities
for light to reach all corners
of an interior.

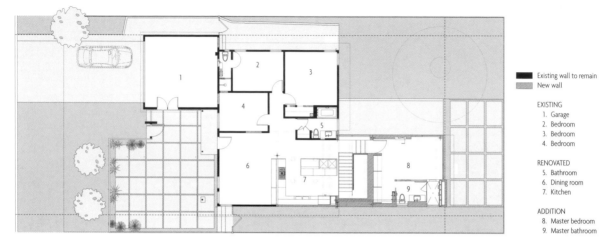

Second-floor plan

■ Existing wall to remain
▨ New wall

EXISTING
1. Garage
2. Bedroom
3. Bedroom
4. Bedroom

RENOVATED
5. Bathroom
6. Dining room
7. Kitchen

ADDITION
8. Master bedroom
9. Master bathroom

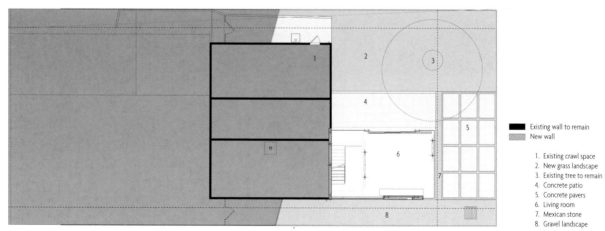

First-floor plan

■ Existing wall to remain
▨ New wall

1. Existing crawl space
2. New grass landscape
3. Existing tree to remain
4. Concrete patio
5. Concrete pavers
6. Living room
7. Mexican stone
8. Gravel landscape

## 073

The building shape can assist cooling by providing self-shading through its deep overhangs and canopies.

The seamless integration of the
extension with the existing house
is enhanced by the long banks of
cabinets and the appliances.

### Vista del Valle

Architects: Zimmerman
and Associates

Location: Sonoma, CA, USA

Photography: © Bruce Damonte

The project's site-responsive design articulates modern forms, while utilizing warm, clean materials that enhance its inviting appeal. A particular design challenge was the preservation of views for neighbors. In response, the house was positioned low in profile on a steep site. The house remains modest in its form from the street, but still creates dramatically lit and inspiring interior spaces that extend out into the landscape.

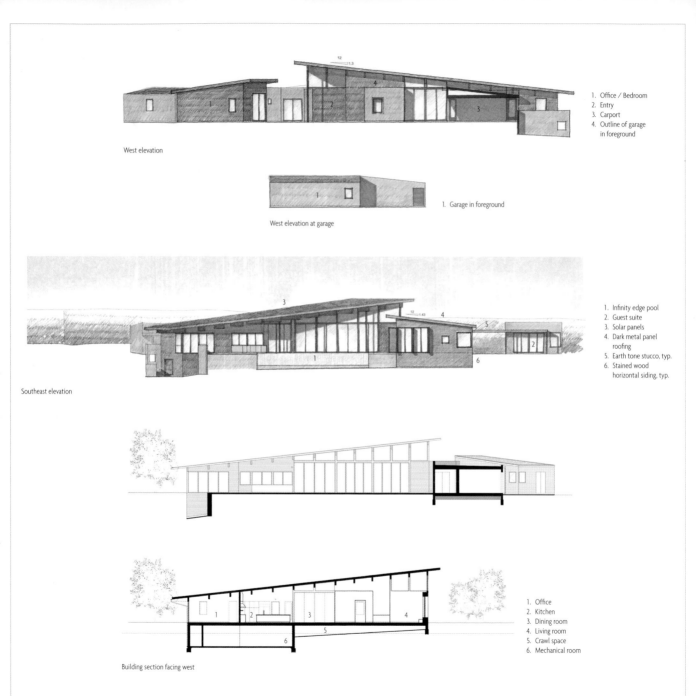

West elevation

1. Office / Bedroom
2. Entry
3. Carport
4. Outline of garage in foreground

West elevation at garage

1. Garage in foreground

Southeast elevation

1. Infinity edge pool
2. Guest suite
3. Solar panels
4. Dark metal panel roofing
5. Earth tone stucco, typ.
6. Stained wood horizontal siding, typ.

Building section facing west

1. Office
2. Kitchen
3. Dining room
4. Living room
5. Crawl space
6. Mechanical room

This 4,200 sq. ft. home complements the beauty of its surrounding landscape with exterior walls of light stucco and warm horizontal cedar siding.

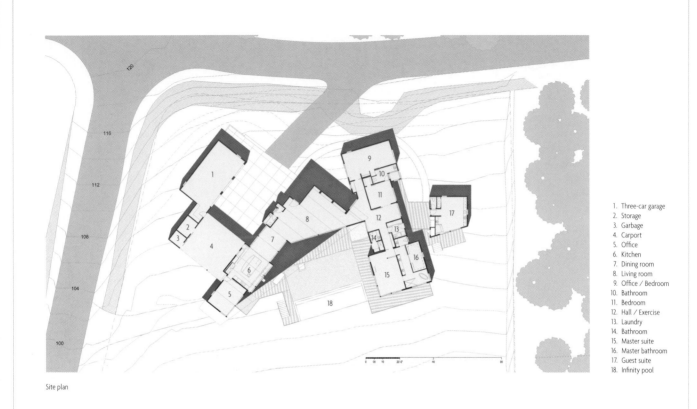

1. Three-car garage
2. Storage
3. Garbage
4. Carport
5. Office
6. Kitchen
7. Dining room
8. Living room
9. Office / Bedroom
10. Bathroom
11. Bedroom
12. Hall / Exercise
13. Laundry
14. Bathroom
15. Master suite
16. Master bathroom
17. Guest suite
18. Infinity pool

The multi-axis plan of this house makes optimum use of the topography and integrates the beauty of the landscape. A thorough study of the sun paths determined the orientation of the building.

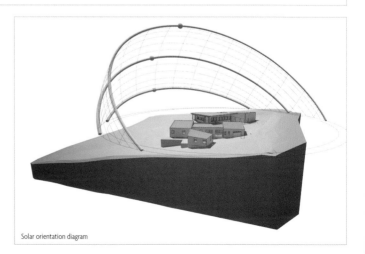

Solar orientation diagram

The project includes a solar hot water heating system and radiant in-floor heating. There is no air-conditioning thanks to a planned solar orientation and passive ventilation.

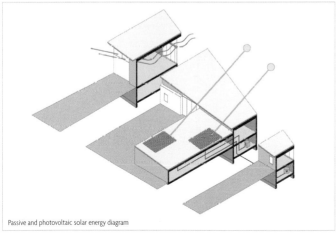

Passive and photovoltaic solar energy diagram

A large roof overhang provides shade
to the kitchen, living, and dining
rooms, allowing the spaces to remain
comfortable year-round.

### Dutchess House #1

The house was conceived of as a country home for occasional use, but it had to be equipped so that it could ultimately evolve into a primary residence. One of the main requests from the client was that the house be open to its beautiful surroundings, yet could be battened down and secured for extended periods. Special attention was paid to sight lines, exposures, seasonal variations in the quality and direction of light, and the flow and integration of interior and exterior spaces.

Architects: Grzywinski+Pons
Location: Millerton, NY, USA
Photography: © Floto + Warner

The house was built with ICFs (insulated concrete forms), strategically glazed with low-E assemblies and clad in high-albedo mill-finish aluminum. Deep eaves were designed based on solar studies.

The matte finish of the aluminum cladding highlights the color variations of the natural surroundings both throughout the day and throughout the seasons.

## 074

A thorough study of the sun and wind paths will help determine the best design of screens and canopies with an emphasis placed on where their openings should sit.

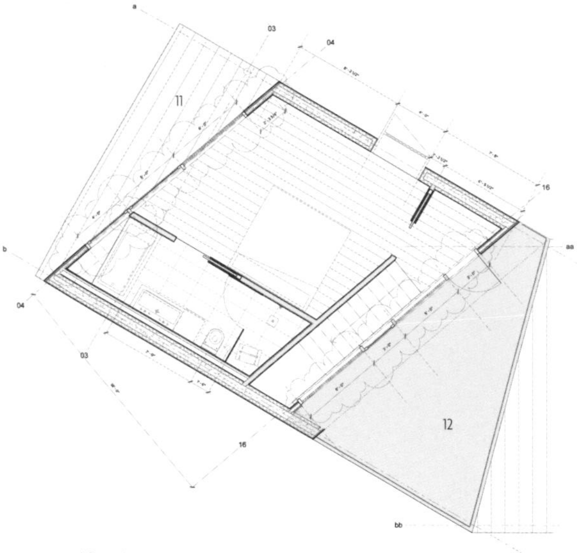

Second-floor plan 1

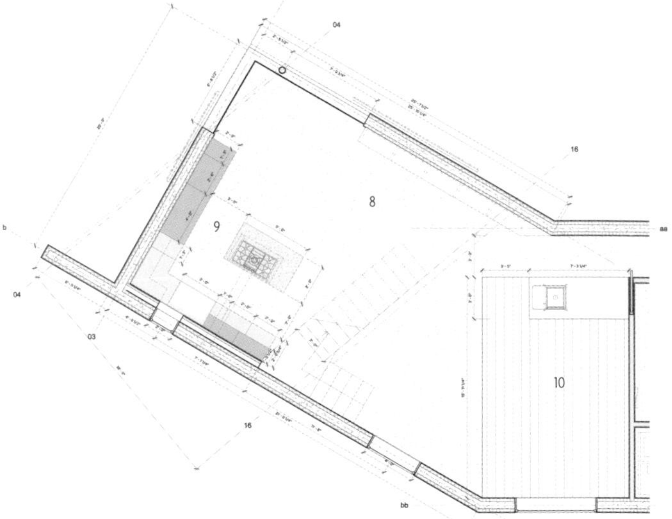

First-floor plan 1

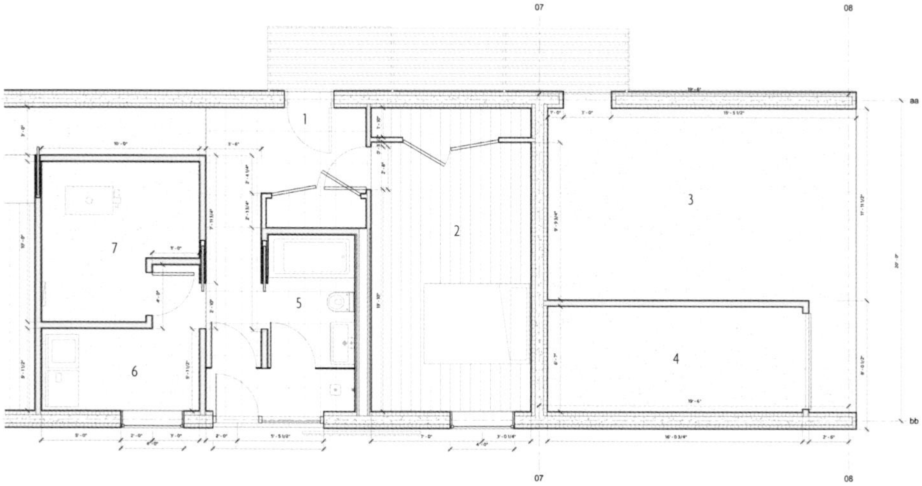

First-floor plan 2

1. Entry
2. Bedroom
3. Garage
4. Landscaping
   equipment storage
5. Bathroom
6. Laundry room
7. Mechanical room
8. Living room
9. Kitchen
10. Dining room
11. Roof
12. Terrace

The home's low-flow fixtures, dual flush toilets, LED lighting, high-efficiency appliances, and sustainably grown lumber were designed to meet the highest sustainability standards.

This single-story house is densely surrounded by residential and office towers. The site is nearly ten feet below street level, leaving the roof as the only light source. Hence, an orthogonal grid of skylights punctures the roof. For privacy purposes, a ceiling made of acrylic vaults under the skylight roof was designed. To enhance the expression of this vaulted ceiling, all interior walls are short of the ceiling.

**Daylight**

Architects: Takeshi Hosaka
Architects
Location: Yokohama, Japan
Photography: © Koji Fujii

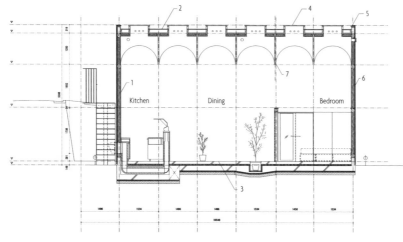

1. Interior finish: Structure board, t = 9mm; osmotic paint white, double coating
2. Roof assembly: Wood deck, t = 20; waterproof urethane, painted; drainage slope 0-60; concrete deck
3. Floor assembly: Dustproof paint; mortar trowel finish, t = 100 mm; insulation / Styrofoam t = 60mm
4. Skylight: Low-E glass t = 4 mm; air t = 12 mm; wire glass t = 6.8 mm
5. Flashing: Galvalume® silver finish
6. Outer wall assembly: Galvalume® silver finish; waterproof sheet; waterproof plasterboard, t = 12.5 mm; structure board t = 12 mm; insulation / glass wool t = 105 mm
7. Ceiling: Acrylite® board, creamy white finish, t = 3 mm

Detailed section

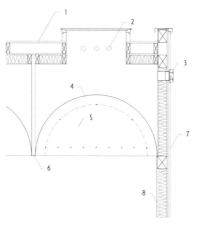

1. FRP waterproofing, t = 3 mm (white coating); silicate calcium board t = 12 mm; plywood t = 12 mm; joist 45 x 45 @ 303; plywood t = 15 mm
2. Hole for attic ventilation
3. Vent cap
4. Acrylite® (acrylic resin, creamy white)
5. Batten for Acrylite®
6. LVL t = 45 mm
7. Galvanized steel sheet
8. Larch plywood t = 9 mm, paint grade finish (white)

Skylight detail

Each room has a window to allow for cross-ventilation. The air space between the roof and the acrylic ceiling exhausts heated air in the summer and serves as a heat buffer in the winter.

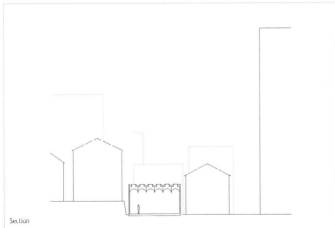

Section

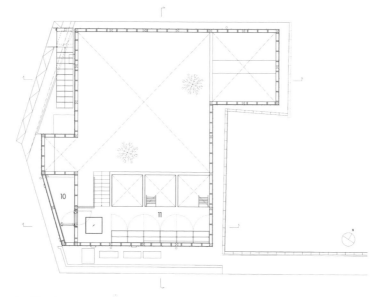

Second-floor plan

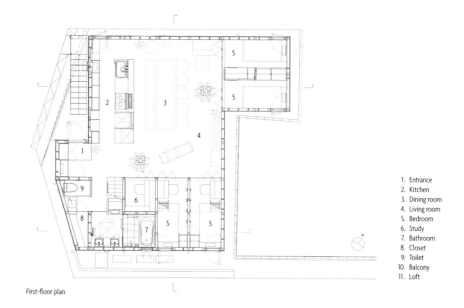

First-floor plan

1. Entrance
2. Kitchen
3. Dining room
4. Living room
5. Bedroom
6. Study
7. Bathroom
8. Closet
9. Toilet
10. Balcony
11. Loft

## 075

Make the most of natural light coming from skylights with partitions that are short of the ceiling for even lighting.

## 076

Translucent screens below skylights help distribute light evenly, minimizing glare and excessive heat gain.

## Byoubugaura House

A house with a basement and two floors aboveground is sandwiched by existing houses to the north and south. On the east, the site faces a ten foot retaining wall. In response, the slabs of all floors are bent upward near the façades to maintain the same window size on all floors. This design attempts to bring air and light to the partially underground basement.

Architects: Takeshi Hosaka
Architects
Location: Yokohama, Japan
Photography: © Koji Fujii

North elevation

West elevation

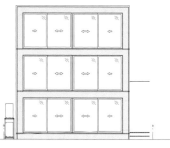

South elevation

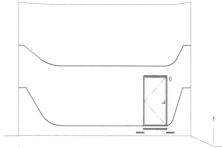

East elevation

# 077

It is important to understand the performance ratings of windows. Before choosing windows for your house, find out what type will work best and where they should be used to optimize energy efficiency.

## 078

Passive solar design decisions are based on building location and climate. These aspects need to be taken into consideration when deciding the orientation and size of windows.

Second-floor plan

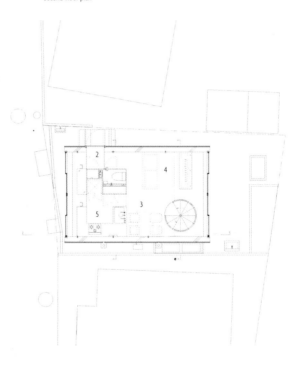

First-floor plan

Basement-floor plan

1. Basement
2. Entrance
3. Dining area
4. Living area
5. Kitchen
6. Bedroom
7. Toilet
8. Bathroom

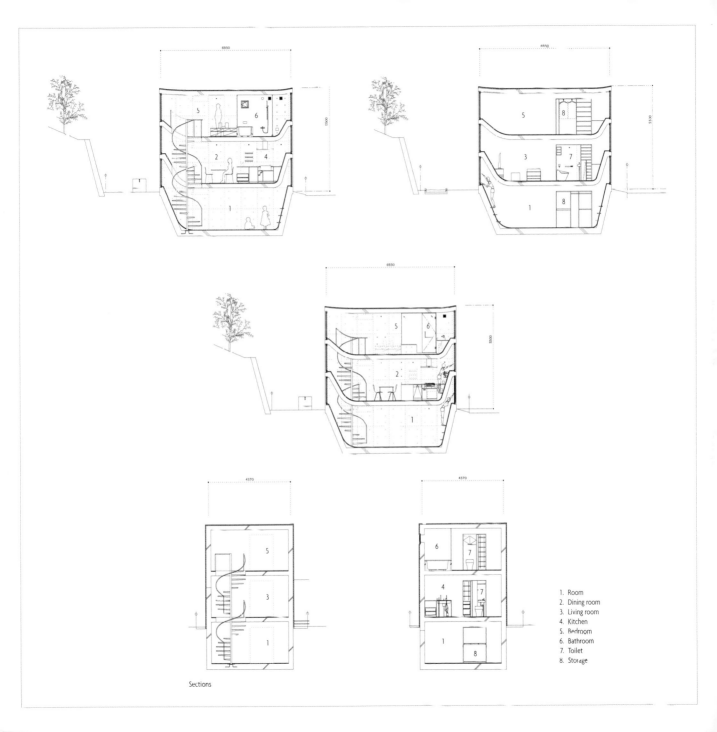

1. Room
2. Dining room
3. Living room
4. Kitchen
5. Bedroom
6. Bathroom
7. Toilet
8. Storage

Sections

The floors slope up to windowsill height,
which at the basement is aligned with the
underside of the floor slab above. This
design decision was meant to block the
view from the street and ensure privacy.

In section, the building maintains the same floor-to-ceiling height, including the basement, which receives light from high above.

## Muallem Residence

In planning this home, emphasis was placed on creating an optimal structure that complied with sustainable design principles. Three major advantages emerge from the positioning of the house on an orthogonal grid, not parallel to the rectangular plot: 1. This positioning achieves an optimal orientation towards the sun. 2. The skewed positioning of the house relative to the plot results in the optimization of the exterior spaces. 3. The positioning enables better views.

Architects: Malka Architects
Location: Israel Valley, Israel
Photography: © Oded Smadar,
Eyal Malka

The concrete entry gate is an off-axis
relative to the house and establishes
a visual relationship with other buildings
along the same street.

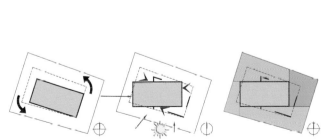

House orientation scheme

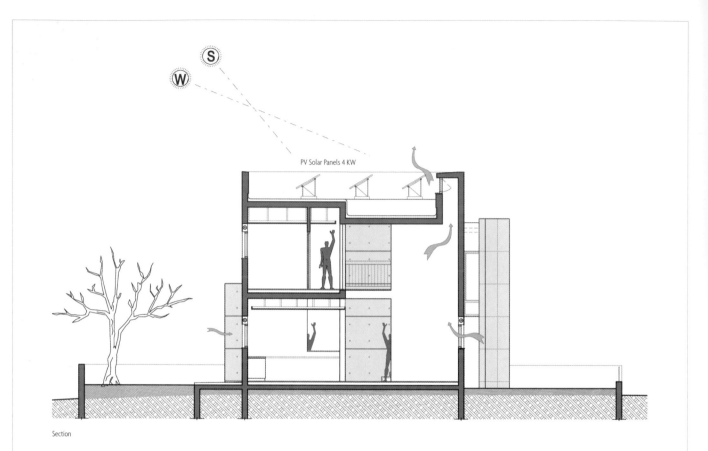

PV Solar Panels 4 KW

Section

# 079

Solar energy is a clean, renewable resource that can be used to heat rooms and water for bathing and cooking.

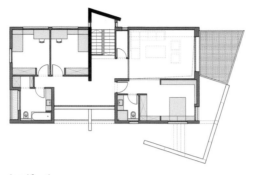

Second-floor plan

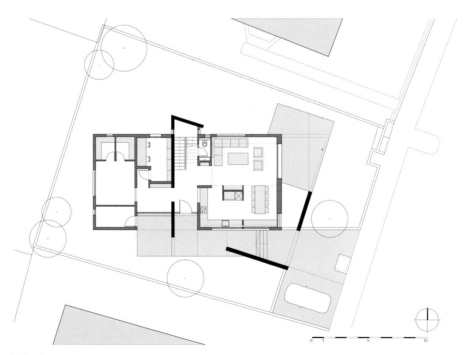

First-floor plan

A "gray flow" system utilizes gray water from the washing machine and bathrooms to irrigate the garden. This system filters the water and distributes it around the garden via a drip-line system.

The house benefits from air-blocks on all four sides and the articulation of spaces allows a natural flow of air.

In this house there is a constant interplay between the immediate environment and the structural expression and tectonics of the design. A courtyard joins the two wings of the house and accommodates the pool, which can be covered by a retractable wooden top, extending over the entertainment area. The deep porch along the north side is typical of South African outdoor living. It provides shade in summer and allows direct sunlight in winter.

Architects: **EFTYCHIS**
Location: Irene, South Africa
Photography: © Emilio Eftychis

## 080

Climate and ecological aspects that are intrinsic to a specific site should be taken into account to ensure climate-appropriate comfort.

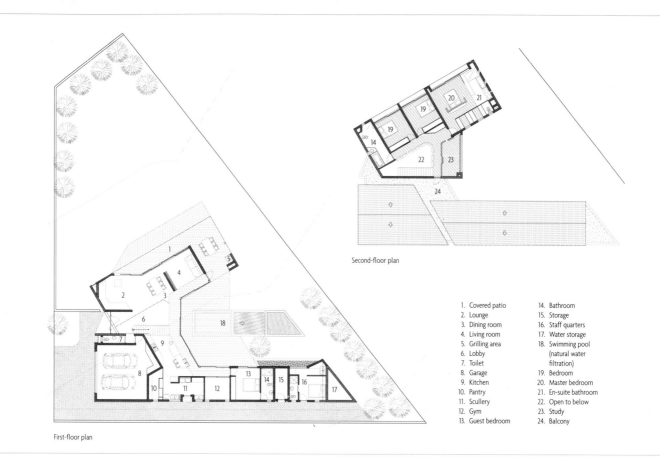

Second-floor plan

First-floor plan

1. Covered patio
2. Lounge
3. Dining room
4. Living room
5. Grilling area
6. Lobby
7. Toilet
8. Garage
9. Kitchen
10. Pantry
11. Scullery
12. Gym
13. Guest bedroom

14. Bathroom
15. Storage
16. Staff quarters
17. Water storage
18. Swimming pool (natural water filtration)
19. Bedroom
20. Master bedroom
21. En-suite bathroom
22. Open to below
23. Study
24. Balcony

The open plan of the living area on the ground floor allows for maximum uninterrupted space that extends into the courtyard, emphasizing the interplay of exterior and interior spaces.

Exposed concrete and corrugated metal cladding evoke the essentials of the understated design: simplicity and purity.

The bio-filters and sand contained in
terraced enclosures filter the pool water,
which is oxygenated by water lilies.

## 081

Appropriate use of exposed
internal thermal mass in
combination with passive
design elements will ensure
that temperature remains
comfortable thanks to
thermal lag.

## 082

For new constructions, consider orienting the kitchen toward the east or southwest, where morning sun will fill it with light.

Architects: Stelle Lomont Rouhani Architects

Location. Water Mill, NY, USA

Photography: © Matthew Carbone, Frank Oudeman

The overall design of this new house was a direct response to a series of environmental regulations, site constraints, solar orientation, and programmatic requirements. It consists of a two-story volume containing bedrooms and baths, and an open, lofty, single-story pavilion. The pavilion was conceived as a breezeway connecting the light and activity of the yard and pool area to the south with the views and wildlife of the pond to the north.

Native, low-maintenance, drought-tolerant landscaping was utilized to transform much of the site from its former suburban, overplanted state to one that calmly coexists with the new structure.

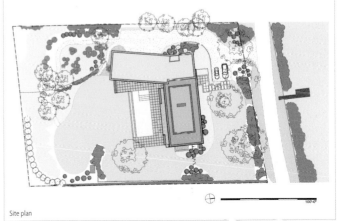

Site plan

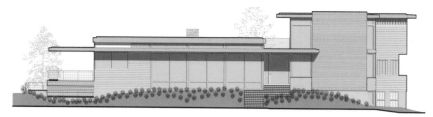

North elevation

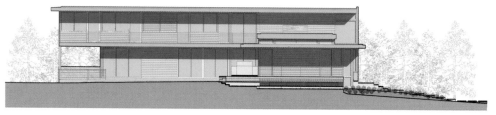

East elevation

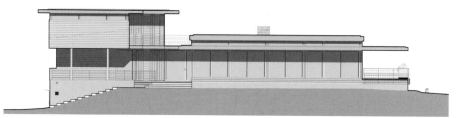

South elevation

West elevation

25'-0"

## 083

A sustainable home must make use of materials that are from sustainable sources, low maintenance, cost effective, and durable.

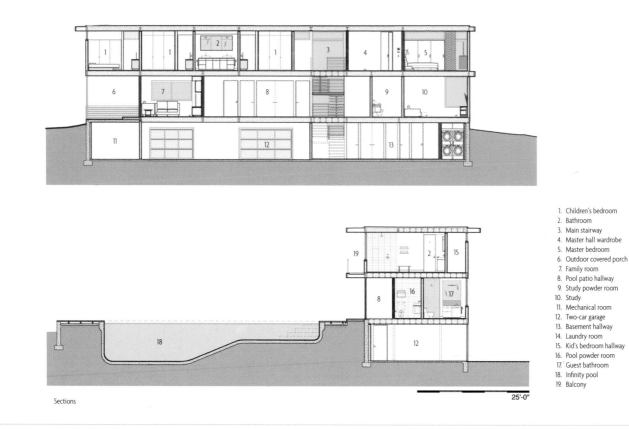

1. Children's bedroom
2. Bathroom
3. Main stairway
4. Master hall wardrobe
5. Master bedroom
6. Outdoor covered porch
7. Family room
8. Pool patio hallway
9. Study powder room
10. Study
11. Mechanical room
12. Two-car garage
13. Basement hallway
14. Laundry room
15. Kid's bedroom hallway
16. Pool powder room
17. Guest bathroom
18. Infinity pool
19. Balcony

Sections

25'-0"

# 084

A house can reduce its heating and cooling costs by using south-facing windows that absorb the sun's energy in order to warm the house in the winter, and large overhangs to keep it cool in the summer.

## 085

Clerestory windows below deep overhangs bring in natural light, minimizing the need for summer air conditioning and allowing solar heat gain in the winter.

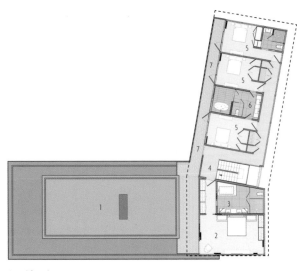

Second-floor plan

1. One-story volume
2. Master bedroom
3. Master bathroom
4. Main stairway
5. Children's bedroom
6. Bathroom
7. Balcony

25'-0"

First-floor plan

1. Front entry patio
2. Entry foyer
3. Living room
4. Dining room
5. Buffet / Wet bar platform
6. Living / Media room stairs
7. Kitchen
8. Study
9. Study powder room
10. Main stairway
11. Guest bedroom
12. Guest bathroom
13. Pool powder room
14. Family room
15. Covered porch
16. Outdoor dining porch
17. Pool deck
18. Pool patio
19. Infinity pool

An efficient heating and cooling system, highly energy efficient glazing, and an advanced building insulation system resulted in a structure that exceeded the requirements of the energy star rating system.

This house remodel harkens back to "old school" kiwi beachside cabins while being a thoroughly modern home. The original two-story 1970s bungalow on the site had little to offer aside from extensive views. The new house retains this quality and provides a modern family home fitting the client's brief. Protection of the environment and the use of eco-friendly materials and systems are integral to the design.

## Lynch Street House

Architects: Dorrington Architects & Associates

Location: Auckland, New Zealand

Photography: © Emma-Jane Hetherington

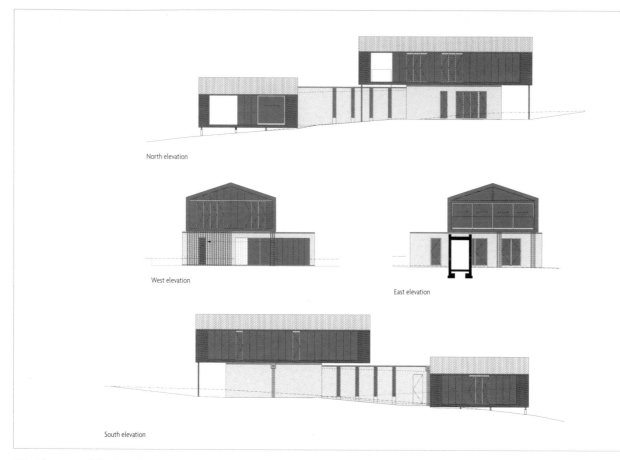

North elevation

West elevation

East elevation

South elevation

Materials were carefully chosen for
energy efficiency, and the architecture
itself complements this ethos.

Second-floor plan

| 12 | 13 |
| 16 | 14 |
| 17 | 15 |
| 8 | |

18

First-floor plan

| 3 | 4 | 5 |
| 1 | | |
| 2 | 6 | 7 |
| 11 | 10 | 9 |
| 8 | 4 | 8 |

1. Entry court
2. Entry gallery / Flexi-space
3. Study
4. Bathroom
5. Bedroom / Flexi-space
6. Gallery
7. Deck
8. Bedroom
9. Service court

10. Laundry / Storage
11. Garage
12. Kitchen
13. Dining room
14. Lounge
15. Deck
16. En-suite bathroom
17. Walk-in closet
18. Planters

The house is composed of a precast
concrete ground floor, a gabled
"boatshed" second floor, and
a separate single-floor timber
"boatshed" at the rear of the plot.

The house uses water collected off the gabled roofs. The roof also supports panels for solar hot water and photovoltaic power generation, with excess electricity fed back into the grid.

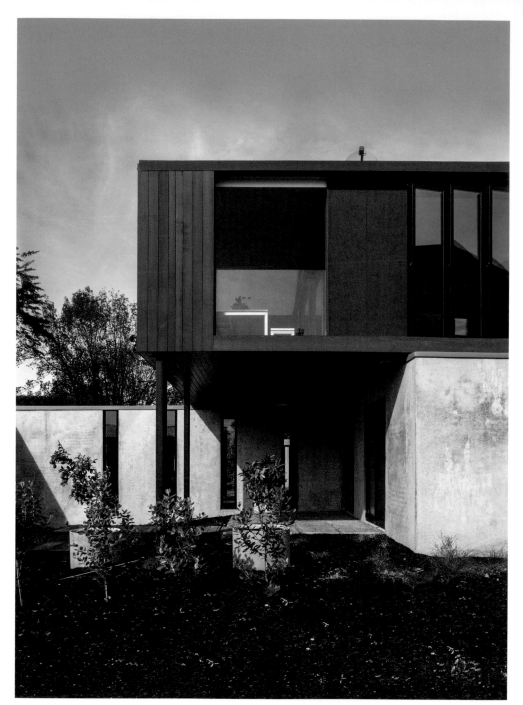

The separate "boatshed" provides a distinct, private space. With its own separate entrance, it can be entirely closed off from the main house.

## 086

In passive solar construction, walls, floors, and roofs take advantage of passive solar gain, collecting, storing, and distributing energy with minimal or no use of mechanical equipment.

Located in the countryside, the 100 square meters (1,076 sq. ft.) house is conceived as a weekend house, easy to use, efficient, and taking full advantage of its natural surroundings. The fluid transition between exterior and interior areas is one of the main characteristics of the project. The house is shaped as a functional cube or, in the words of the architects, a "living box" that can be opened, closed, switched on, heated, and cooled down easily and rapidly.

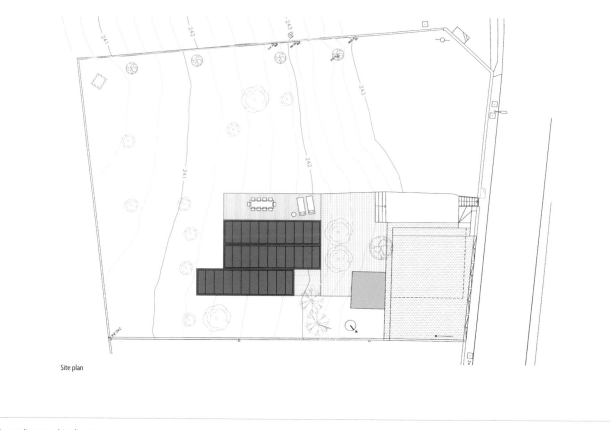

Site plan

The project relies on a bioclimatic
architecture, adapting the form and
positioning of the house to its energetic
needs: natural ventilation, passive solar
design, intelligent façade system, and
natural shade.

## 087

Modular construction is cost effective because most of the construction takes place in a workshop. This minimizes on-site waste production and reduces mounting and dismounting time.

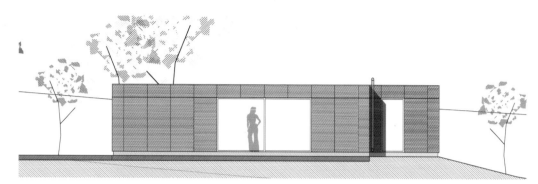

South elevation

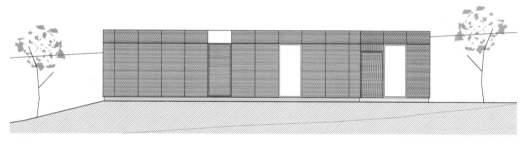

North elevation

## 088

A bioclimatic design, the use of eco-friendly materials, and the utilization of renewable energies contribute to a highly efficient sustainable house.

## 089

An east orientation will benefit from the morning sun, but will leave the west wall more exposed to overheating. This factor should be taken into account when placing windows.

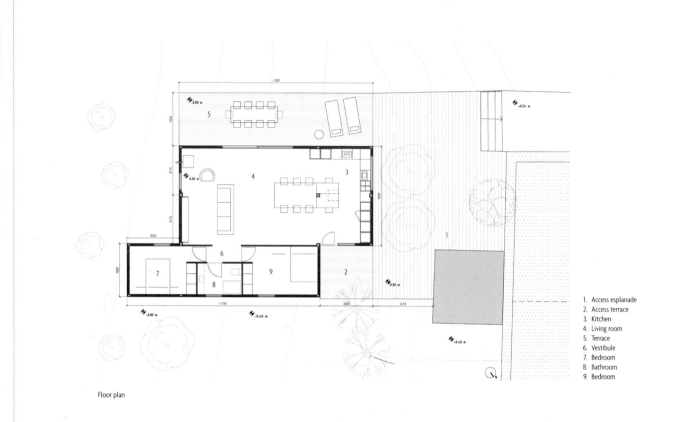

Floor plan

1. Access esplanade
2. Access terrace
3. Kitchen
4. Living room
5. Terrace
6. Vestibule
7. Bedroom
8. Bathroom
9. Bedroom

# 090

Generally, to take full advantage of sun exposure, buildings should have their long sides oriented along an east-west axis. This means that most windows should face south.

## 091

In addition to complementing
a building's structure
and defining its aesthetic
appearance, exterior wall
finishes make a major
contribution to sustainability.

The shutters play an important role both for the aesthetic value of the house and its energy efficiency. The shutters, which are integrated in the façade, use perforated panels of Corten® steel.

El Tiemblo House
"Raulinski"

Architects: James & Mau
Location: El Tiemblo, Spain
Photography: © Pablo Sarabia

The project is based on a bioclimatic and modular design representing the key values of the Infiniski brand. Its prefabrication process allowed for a reduction in costs, time, and environmental impact; and due to its modularity, the house can not only be customized, but also be easily enlarged to satisfy the needs of its occupants. El Tiemblo House is composed of four recycled steel shipping containers forming an L-shape to take full advantage of the topographic setting, light, and views.

# 092

While steel may not be the most environmentally friendly material, it does have some sustainable advantages: resource efficiency, recyclability, low waste production, and off-site manufacturing.

## 093

Because steel is a fast, safe construction material, its use reduces work time, thereby lowering costs for the homeowners.

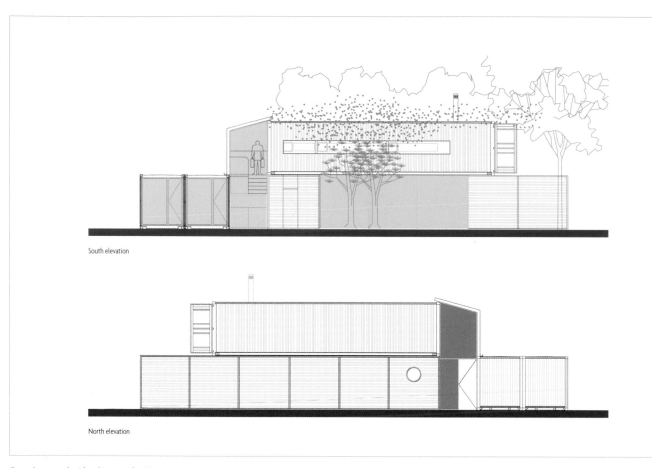

South elevation

North elevation

Complemented with a biomass heating system, the house achieves high energy efficiency during winter. In summer, climbing plants create a natural solar protection and a ventilated thermal envelope.

## 094

Steel constructions are usually light, airy, and adaptable, and just as easy to take down as to build. This quality permits easy modifications of them.

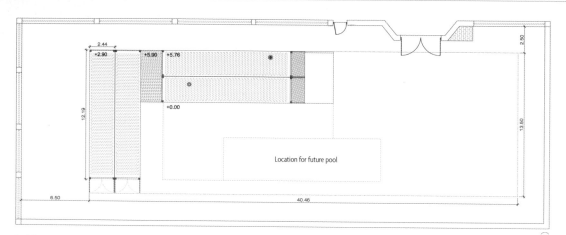

2.44

+2.90   +5.90   +5.76

+0.00

12.19

2.50

13.50

Location for future pool

6.50   40.46

Roof plan

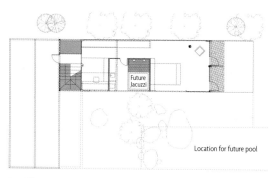

Future
Jacuzzi

Location for future pool

Second-floor plan

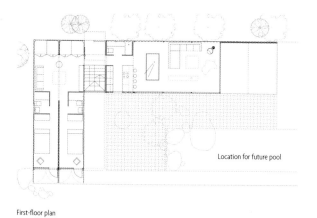

Location for future pool

First-floor plan

The shape and size of the containers are no obstacle to creating comfort. Arranged on one floor or stacked up, the steel containers can be arranged in any desired configuration.

## 095

The level of insulation in walls, floors, and ceilings can affect the amount of heat transfer in and out of the house.

## Pinus House

This house is located at 1,800 meters (5,905 feet) above sea level and is surrounded by forests of native pines. It does not alter the steep topography of the landscape, but actually enhances it. The climatic characteristics of the mountainous region where the house is located guided the design strategies to optimize energy use in a passive way and to minimize the environmental impact of the construction.

Architect: André Eisenlohr
Location: Campos do Jordão, Brazil
Photography: © André Eisenlohr

Eucalyptus, pine, garapa, and
muiracatiara timber were harvested
in areas of reforestation.

The body of the house was built off the ground by means of eucalyptus pillars, which prevent moisture from the soil affecting the floor.

## 096

The stilt construction method has a minimal impact on the landscape because of the small area of construction in contact with the ground. Also, because the house is elevated, surface runoff is not affected.

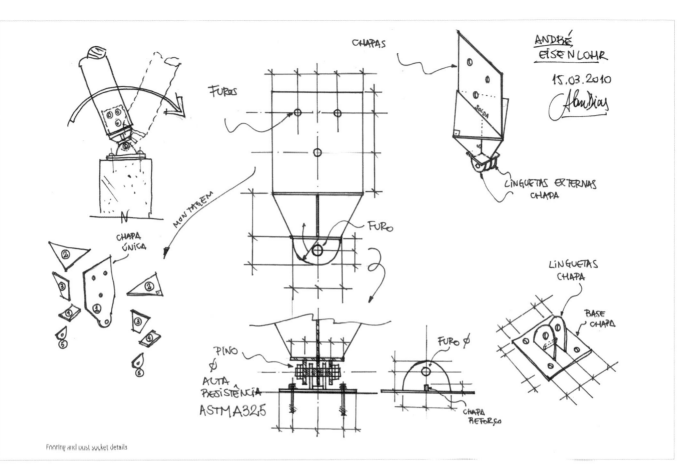

Footing and post socket details

097

Concrete footings can prevent ground moisture from rising through wood structural components by capillarity.

The thermal insulation of the house is
made of expanded polystyrene that was
collected from various construction sites
and reused.

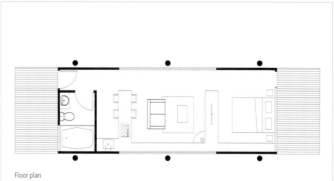

Floor plan

## 098

The wood residue generated during construction can be reused to produce OSB (oriented strand board) panels. These can be used to build interior partitions and furniture.

## Eucalyptus House

Located on a steep sloping terrain in a forest reserve, this 50 square meter (538 sq. ft.) house has large south-facing windows and a balcony. The design incorporates materials and construction techniques that minimize environmental impact. The use of energy-efficiency strategies such as passive solar energy and high thermal insulation give the house a unique appeal.

Architect: André Eisenlohr
Location: Campos do Jordão, Brazil
Photography: © André Eisenlohr

The wood structure of the house is reinforced with steel cables bracing the construction against lateral loading and overturning.

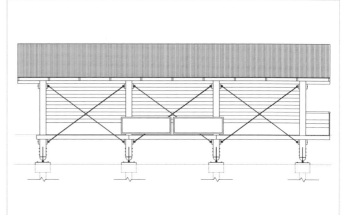

North elevation

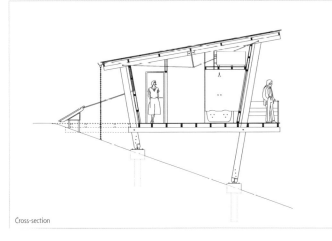

Cross-section

## 099

South-facing windows should be as large as possible to maximize solar gain.

Most of the leftover material was reused for the production of the kitchen cabinets and countertops, as well as for furniture.

## 100

Small houses are inherently energy efficient as they use fewer resources, both in their construction and maintenance than larger houses do. This translates into a lower environmental impact.

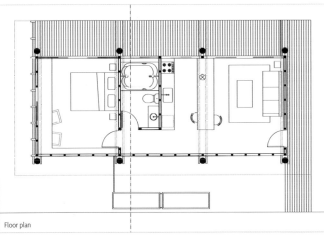

Floor plan

For the architects of this home it was important not to destroy the magnificent landscape of the Douro Valley, classified as a world heritage site by UNESCO and land of the extraordinary vines that produce the well-known Porto wine. Hence, the house, with a green roof, is completely integrated into the existing cultivated landscape. All the rooms have their views directed to the Douro River except the kitchen and the hall that lead to two sunken courtyards.

**Douro Valley
Sustainable House**

Architects· Utopia
Arquitectura e Engenharia

Location: Sabrosa, Portugal

Photography: © Utopia
Arquitectura e Engenharia

# 101

Green roofs are an efficient and environmentally friendly design solution to facilitate the integration of a building into the landscape.

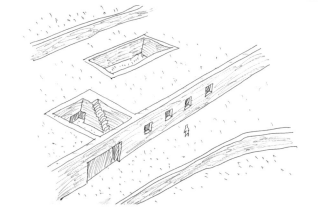

Design sketch

Shale extracted from the earth was used to build the thick exterior walls. This meant a reduction of carbon dioxide emissions on transportations. The green roofs are planted with indigenous grasses.

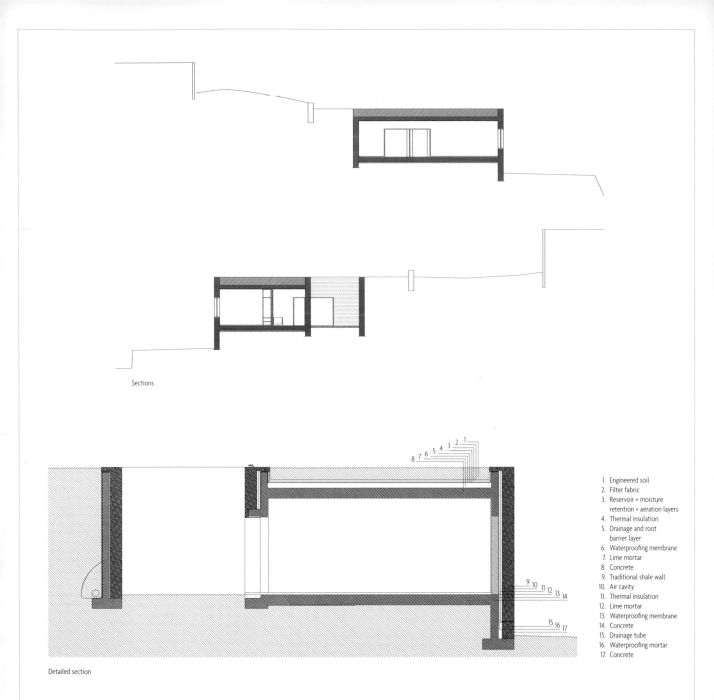

Sections

Detailed section

1. Engineered soil
2. Filter fabric
3. Reservoir + moisture retention + aeration layers
4. Thermal insulation
5. Drainage and root barrier layer
6. Waterproofing membrane
7. Lime mortar
8. Concrete
9. Traditional shale wall
10. Air cavity
11. Thermal insulation
12. Lime mortar
13. Waterproofing membrane
14. Concrete
15. Drainage tube
16. Waterproofing mortar
17. Concrete

## 102

The natural sloping profile of a site can be used to create sunken courtyards offering a shaded microclimate that will result in a cooling effect.

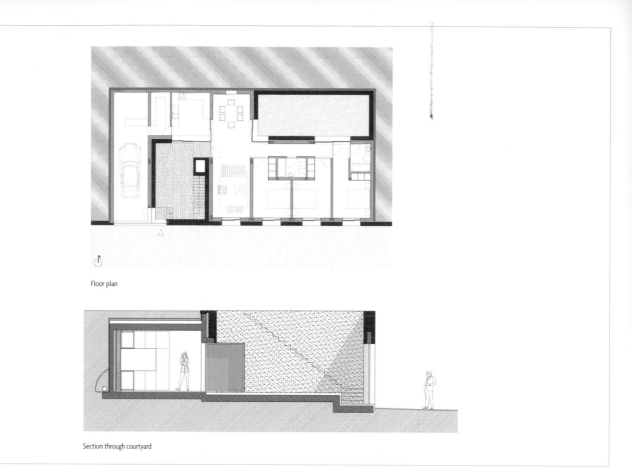

Floor plan

Section through courtyard

## 103

Maximizing the surface
of a building in contact with
the ground helps minimize
temperature swing, since
the ground provides very
low thermal amplitude.

## 104

The reflectivity of interior finishes is an important factor to take into account early in the design process of a home in order to optimize energy use.

## Oblio House

Oblio House is a study on the relationship between circulation and topography, reinterpreting traditional vernacular styles of New Mexico in a contemporary manner. Built on a steep hill, the design organizes the house on two levels that step down the site. The house utilizes passive solar photovoltaic and hot water roof panels for electricity and radiant heating. Rainwater is collected in underground cisterns for landscape irrigation.

Architects: Edward Fitzgerald / Architects

Location: Albuquerque, NM, USA

Photography: © Robert Reck Photography

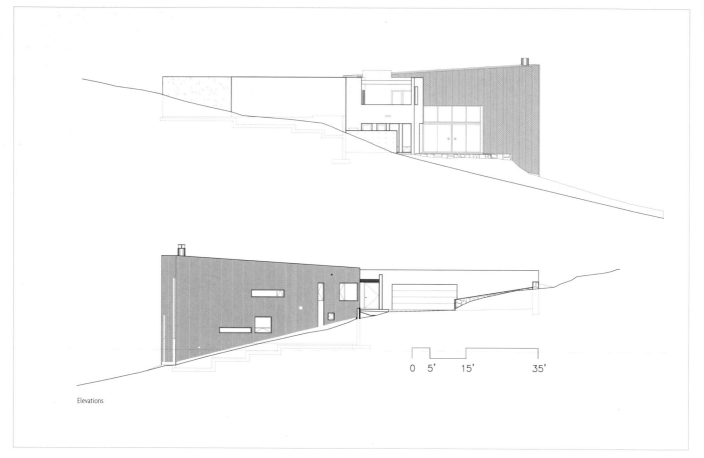

Elevations

| | | | |
|---|---|---|---|
| 0 | 5' | 15' | 35' |

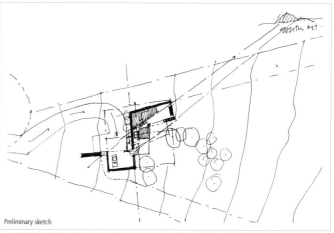

Preliminary sketch

## 105

Two wings forming an angle create a protected outdoor area that minimizes the boundaries between interior and exterior.

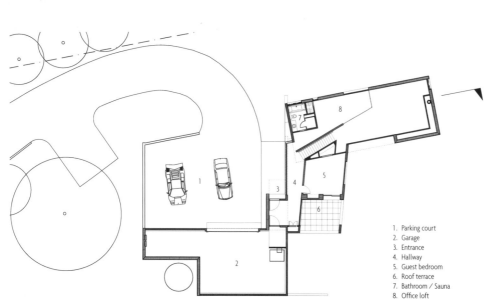

Ground-floor plan

1. Parking court
2. Garage
3. Entrance
4. Hallway
5. Guest bedroom
6. Roof terrace
7. Bathroom / Sauna
8. Office loft

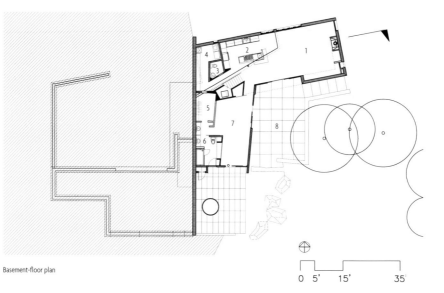

Basement-floor plan

1. Living and dining room
2. Kitchen
3. Powder room
4. Laundry
5. Closet
6. Master bathroom
7. Master bedroom
8. Terrace

0  5'  15'  35'

The house has polished concrete floors, insulated concrete forms (ICF), and recycled wood stud framing. Exterior finishes include stucco, a corrugated metal roof, and wall panels.

## 106

Window size and spacing, type of glazing, reflectance of finishes, and location of interior partitions should be carefully evaluated to make the most of natural lighting.

## 107

Low-flow technology has fitted bathroom fixtures with devices that decrease the amount of water used by pushing air into the stream of water.

## HUF House ART 5

HUF House ART 5 is an example of the successful range of energy-efficient homes that HUF HAUS strives to develop, taking into consideration land conditions, climate, and budget. HUF House ART 5 is a modern post-and-beam structure with generous amounts of glass that makes for a unique living space surrounded by nature.

Architects: HUF HAUS
Location: Cologne, Germany
Photography: © HUF HAUS

The basement of the HUF House ART 5 accommodates an innovative energy storage solution. The equipment runs with a high-performance lithium ion battery.

## 108

There are general limitations in the amount of glass that can be used in the construction of a home. This amount can be exceeded, however, if the increased use of glass can improve energy efficiency.

## 109

When it comes to interior finishes, it is best to choose products and materials that minimize the amount of harmful substances you are exposed to.

Second-floor plan

1. Gallery
2. Master bedroom
3. Dressing area
4. Sauna
5. Bathroom
6. Bedroom
7. Bedroom

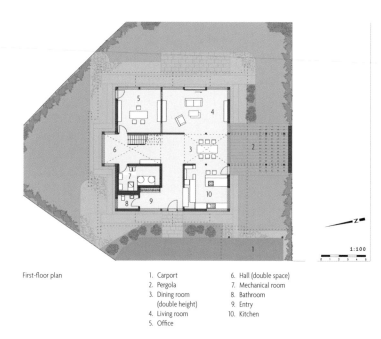

First-floor plan

1. Carport
2. Pergola
3. Dining room
   (double height)
4. Living room
5. Office
6. Hall (double space)
7. Mechanical room
8. Bathroom
9. Entry
10. Kitchen

1:100

## 110

Using natural lighting strategies and choosing energy-efficient light fixtures can help reduce electricity use and lower energy bills.

This is the site of a ruined farm where all that remained when the project began were outside walls and an adjacent chalet. Thinking creatively, the architects realized these elements offered the chance to build a structure that was both a vernacular architectural presence and would fulfill a contemporary desire for sustainable architecture informed by recent technological developments.

Architects: Atelier d'Architecture Christian Girard
Location: Villaroger, France
Photography: © Nicolas Borel

Earthquake and avalanche protection
methods were integrated into the
structural design of Mineral Lodge, which
is located high up in the French Alps.

East-west section

0          5

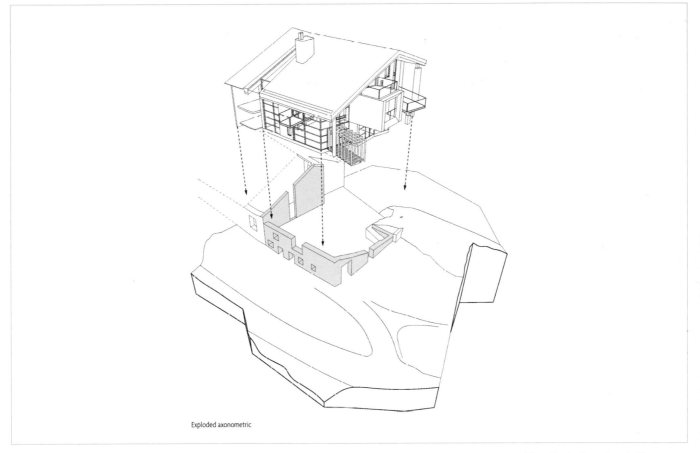

Exploded axonometric

Mineral Lodge is equipped with geothermal heating provided by a heat pump. It circulates water in three 150-meter-deep drills in rock where temperature is stable all year around.

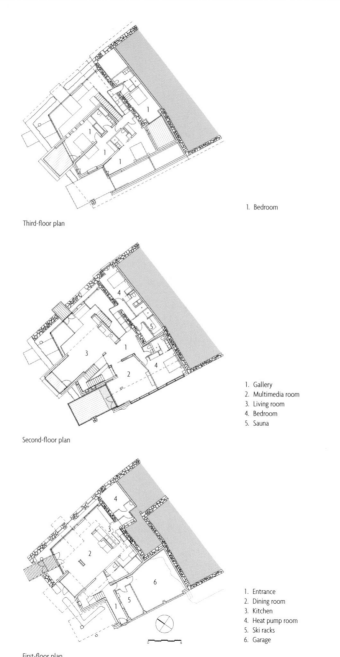

1. Bedroom

Third-floor plan

1. Gallery
2. Multimedia room
3. Living room
4. Bedroom
5. Sauna

Second-floor plan

1. Entrance
2. Dining room
3. Kitchen
4. Heat pump room
5. Ski racks
6. Garage

First-floor plan

The new construction allows light into the house through windows made of high quality glass and frames.

## 111

Effective use of daylight
depends on a range of factors,
including the sun's altitude and
azimuth; the relative occurrence
of overcast versus sunny
weather; the season; and
levels of pollution and haze.

The architects and owners of this house infused it with both New Zealand and Japanese influences. The design of the building took into consideration the sloping terrain, orientation for best views, sun exposure, and protection from prevailing winds. With energy efficiency and cost effectiveness in mind, the architects utilized new materials and techniques to ensure that the house would be comfortable all year round.

### Broad Oaks Showhome

Architects: Bob Burnett Architecture

Location: Christchurch, New Zealand

Photography: © Bob Burnett

## 112

To reduce energy costs and to contribute to global energy efficiency, windows are a good place to start. Double-glazed windows with argon gas low-E glass provide good insulation against heat transfer.

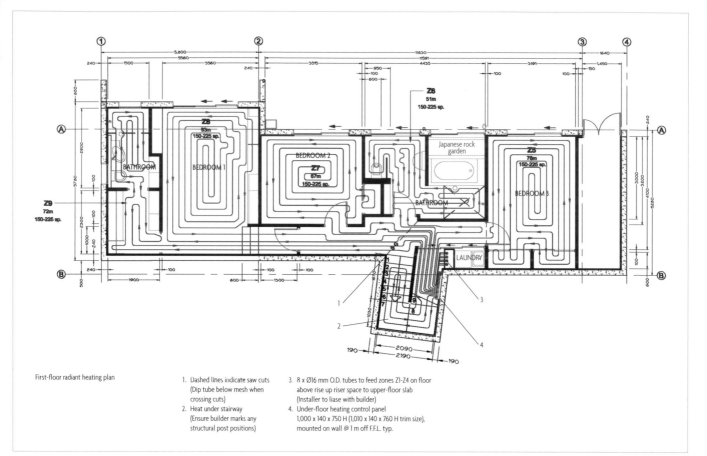

First-floor radiant heating plan

1. Dashed lines indicate saw cuts
   (Dip tube below mesh when
   crossing cuts)
2. Heat under stairway
   (Ensure builder marks any
   structural post positions)

3. 8 x Ø16 mm O.D. tubes to feed zones Z1–Z4 on floor
   above rise up riser space to upper-floor slab
   (Installer to liase with builder)
4. Under-floor heating control panel
   1,000 x 140 x 750 H (1,010 x 140 x 760 H trim size),
   mounted on wall @ 1 m off F.F.L. typ.

The lower and intermediate floors are concrete and have water reticulated under-floor heating. This hydronic system was installed with energy efficiency in mind, as it uses little electricity and can be powered by solar water heaters.

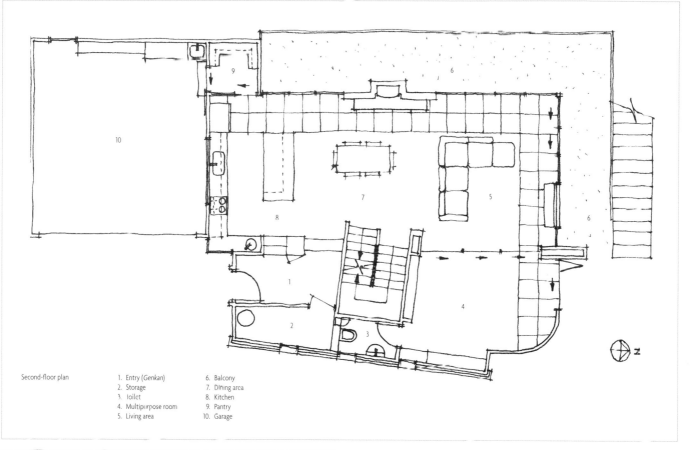

Second-floor plan

1. Entry (*Genkan*)
2. Storage
3. Toilet
4. Multipurpose room
5. Living area
6. Balcony
7. Dining area
8. Kitchen
9. Pantry
10. Garage

The house interior is lined with GIB
Ultraline® Plus gypboard, which is
manufactured in New Zealand for
New Zealand's climate conditions and
provides additional density and rigidity.

## 113

Bamboo flooring is produced from a fast-growing renewable natural material that has antibacterial properties and is water resistant. These qualities make bamboo a sustainable alternative to hardwoods.

Bridge House is a long, narrow, two-story building with a design made to look like the lower level is submerged and only revealed through a saddle. The upper level is completely visible and bridges two man-made mounds. The project deals both with architecture and with landscape design. Taking into account sustainable principles, the house can generate its own energy, making it possible for the occupants to go off-grid at any time.

## Bridge House

Architects: 123DV Modern Villas

Location: Rotterdam, the Netherlands

Photography: © Christiaan de Bruijne

The house uses Heat Mirror® insulating glass. This unique material acts as an efficient and environmentally friendly temperature regulator, cooling the house and preventing excessive heating.

## 114

Heat Mirror® insulating glass is composed of a heat-reflective coating with two internal air chambers to mitigate conductive and radiated heat flow.

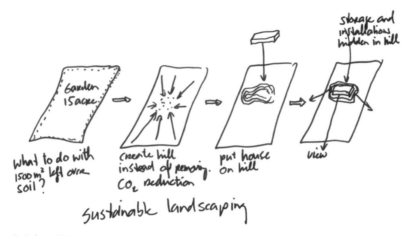

storage and installations hidden in hill

Garden 15 acre.

what to do with 1500 m² left over soil?

create hill instead of removing. $CO_2$ reduction

put house on hill

view

sustainable landscaping

Sketch of sustainable landscaping

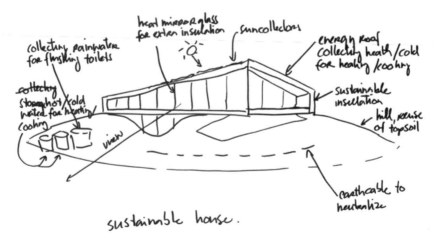

heat mirror glass for exter insulation

suncollectors

energy roof collecting heath/cold for heating/cooling

collecting rainwater for flushing toilets

sustainable insulation

collecting storage hot/cold water for heating cooling

hill, reuse of topsoil

view

earthcable to neutralize

sustainable house.

liong lie

Sketch of environmental systems

The practical and sustainable features include roof and floor heating through thermal energy storage, reuse of rainwater, a septic tank, and photovoltaic panels on the roof.

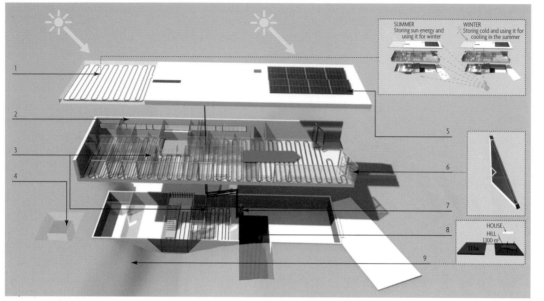

1. COLLECTING SUN ENERGY
   Energy roof
2. FIBER BOARD MADE OUT OF WASTE WOOD FROM SUSTAINABLE FORESTS
   Pavatex Diffutherm™ insulation system
3. FLOOR HEATING/COOLING
4. COLLECTING RAINWATER FOR INSIDE USE
   Water tank
5. USING SUN ENERGY TO PRODUCE ELECTRICITY
   Solar panels
6. MIRRORING SUN HEAT
   Special double glass with membrane
7. MULTILAYER BOILER
8. COLLECTING EARTH HEAT OR COLD
   Thermal storage system
9. LAND CULTIVATION requires removing top soil (1,100 m³) and creating a hill. The top soil is kept on site ($CO_2$ reduction)

HOUSE
HILL
1,100 m³
13 ha

Exploded axonometric. Environmental systems diagram

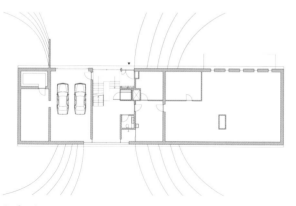

First-floor plan

Second-floor plan

## 115

Perfecting the use of glass windows encourages sustainability, as a high percentage of energy flows in and out of a building through its windows.

## 116

The well-designed placement of windows, skylights, and artificial lighting is critical to minimize energy consumption. When done incorrectly, occupants deal with glare and thermal discomfort.

## 117

Large sliding doors on opposite walls provide ample cross-ventilation to cool a house on warm days. Both light sources combine to make an evenly lit interior.

A sloping terrain at the foot of a hill made this a challenging site to accommodate a house and simultaneously integrate it into the landscape. Yet the architects were able to do this and give the home panoramic views. The structure, which is entirely built with timber panels, also meets the requirements for both winter and summer insulation and for healthy living conditions. The design of the house reflects the occupants' passion for art and graphic design.

Architects: Philipp Architekten
Location: Balingen, Germany
Photography: © Philipp Architekten, Udo Geisler

## 118

Deep overhangs serve as
solar protection, creating a
microclimate around a house
and allowing outdoor activities
to take place in comfortable
conditions.

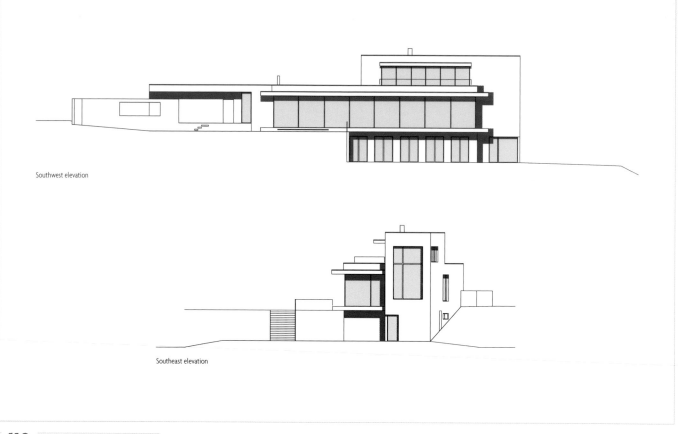

Southwest elevation

Southeast elevation

## 119

Choose naturally occurring flat
areas or gently sloped parts
of a site to minimize disruption
of the landscape.

Carefully evaluate topography, building proportions, setbacks, landscape design, vehicle access, and energy-efficiency possibilities.

# 121

A rectangular building with one of its long façades facing south can allow for high solar heating, sunlight, and natural ventilation.

Organize the interior layout of the home to make the most of daylight, locating the most-used rooms on the south side and the least-used rooms on the north side.

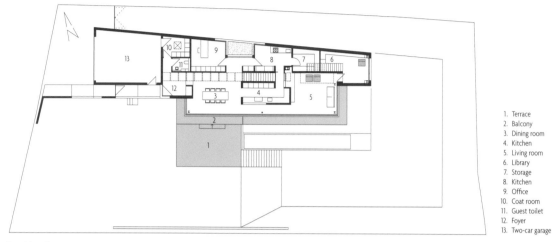

Second-floor plan

1. Terrace
2. Balcony
3. Dining room
4. Kitchen
5. Living room
6. Library
7. Storage
8. Kitchen
9. Office
10. Coat room
11. Guest toilet
12. Foyer
13. Two-car garage

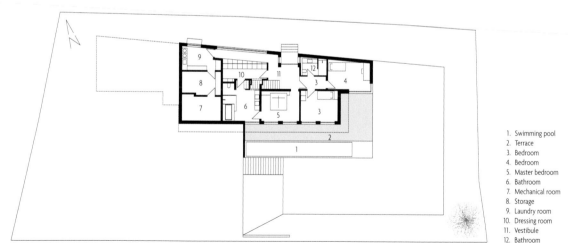

First-floor plan

1. Swimming pool
2. Terrace
3. Bedroom
4. Bedroom
5. Master bedroom
6. Bathroom
7. Mechanical room
8. Storage
9. Laundry room
10. Dressing room
11. Vestibule
12. Bathroom

## 123

Using energy-efficient light bulbs will optimize artificial lighting and reduce electricity costs.

Located on a mountain ridge in southern Germany, House P is formed by a central glazed cube. A wood-paneled core within this glass cube has utilitarian functions and acts as the backbone for the second floor. A minimalist approach, featuring white plaster finishes, was brought to the design of the house. This minimalist aesthetic extends from beyond the walls of the house to the design of the landscape.

## House P

Architects: Philipp Architekten
Location: Waldenburg, Germany
Photography: © Johannes Kottjé,
Victor Brigola, Oliver Schuster

## 124

Color can play an important
role in passive cooling.
Light-colored surfaces reflect
light and heat, while dark
colors absorb radiant energy.

Second-floor plan

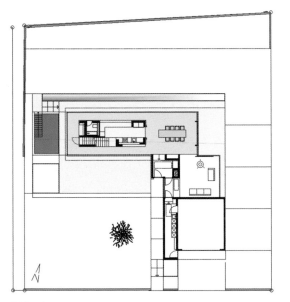

First-floor plan

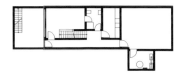

Basement-floor plan

The presence of water can produce a cooling effect. That is why water features are in courtyards located in hot, dry climates.

## 126

Shading by means of deep overhangs is perhaps the simplest cooling form. Other cooling options involve the strategic planting of trees, vines, and shrubs.

High levels of insulation in
walls, ceilings, and a roof,
energy-efficient windows,
and low levels of air infiltration
contribute to the optimization
of energy performance.

**Hollis House**

Architects: Silva Studios Architecture

Location: Poway, CA, USA

Photography: © James Jaeger Photography

This seven thousand sq. ft. environmentally responsible home has views in all directions. The effect captures natural seasonal breezes, daylight throughout the home's interior, and drought-resistant native landscaping. It features 20 KW, PV (photovoltaic) solar technology, solar hot water, rainwater collection, and gray water collection. It is framed with recyclable steel, 100 percent cotton insulation (made from recycled blue jeans), and cabinets of sustainably grown Lyptus wood. It is fire resistant inside and out.

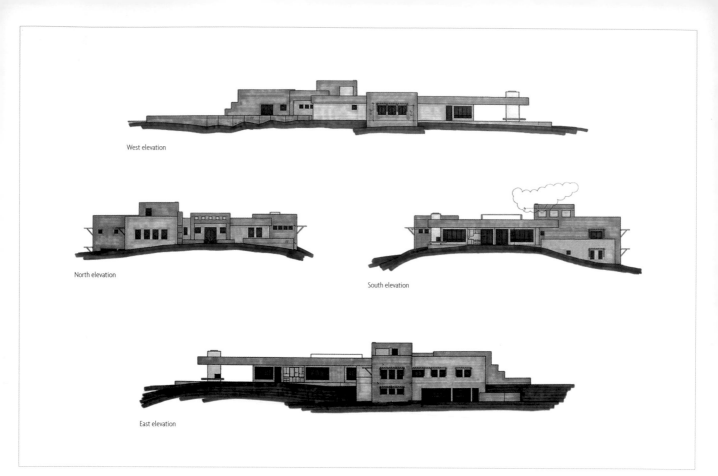

West elevation

North elevation

South elevation

East elevation

The building planning and massing should make the most of the buildable area of the site with a minimal impact on the environment.

## 129

The optimal size of canopies and overhangs depends on the site's location and climate.

The selection of materials applied to exterior walls should be decided based on their environmental performance. The criteria can relate to their sourcing, maintenance, and disposal.

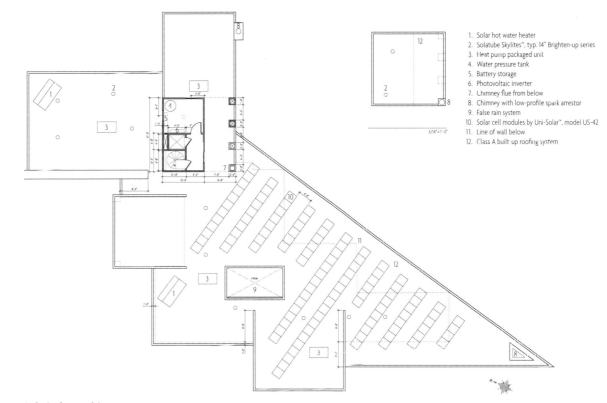

1. Solar hot water heater
2. Solatube Skylites™, typ. 14" Brighten-up series
3. Heat pump packaged unit
4. Water pressure tank
5. Battery storage
6. Photovoltaic inverter
7. Chimney flue from below
8. Chimney with low-profile spark arrestor
9. False rain system
10. Solar cell modules by Uni-Solar™, model US-42
11. Line of wall below
12. Class A built-up roofing system

3/16"=1'-0"

Roof and roof access roof plan

## 131

Adopting energy-efficient strategies, such as the use of renewable energy, will lower energy costs and, as environmental awareness grows, will add value to your property.

Hollis House **435**

## 132

When deciding the orientation of your home take into account the location of landscape features on your site. These features may have an impact on how you harness sunlight.

## 133

In a long narrow space, gallery kitchens are most efficient when oriented toward a bank of windows to optimize natural lighting.

Bio Domus D.01

Bio Domus D.01 revisits Mediterranean architecture with a minimalist approach that follows concepts of bio-architecture. It embraces the eco-friendly practices of sustainable construction, permaculture (a branch of ecological design), eco-engineering, and environmental design based on sustainable architecture systems modeled after natural systems. It utilizes natural materials, as well as the energy-conscious practices of geometry, sacred geometry, and feng shui.

Architects: Aroma Italiano
Location: San José, Costa Rica
Photography: © Aroma Italiano

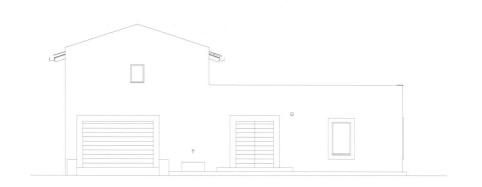

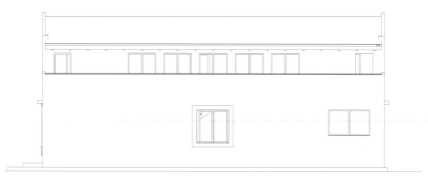

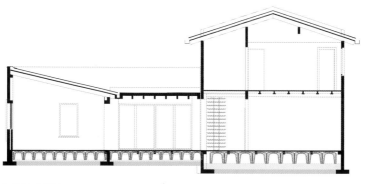

Elevations and section

The house is open, simple, and dynamic, inspired by the building concepts of the Roman *domus*: white surfaces, stone, open spaces, and a central courtyard with a water feature.

Ventilated and
dry roof

Healthy and dry
environment

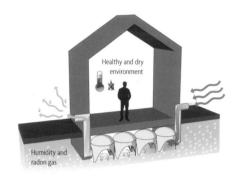

Healthy and dry
environment

Humidity and
radon gas

Energy savings

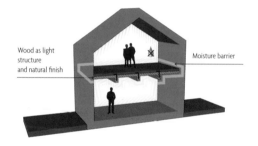

Wood as light
structure
and natural finish

Moisture barrier

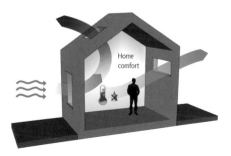

Home
comfort

Healthy and dry
environment

Environmental system diagrams

New technologies combine with traditional construction methods to create a unique house. The use of eco-friendly materials and systems allow energy saving, ensuring a long-lasting, healthy dwelling.

Architects: Takeshi Hosaka
Architects
Location: Katsushika,
Tokyo, Japan
Photography: © Koji Fujii

The irregular quadrangular shape of the site dictates the overall footprint of the two-story high building. The design was conceived as a "house within a house" with an interstitial outdoor space separating them. The roof and wall sides of the volume have carefully designed openings that let light and air in, while the open space that surrounds the inner house serves as a temperature regulator.

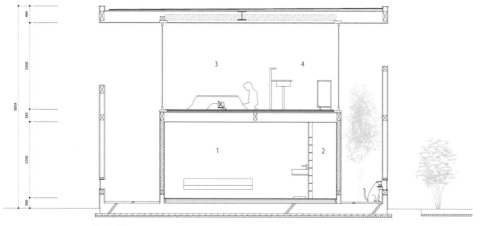

Section AA'

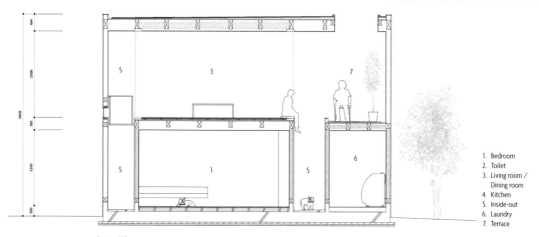

Section BB'

1. Bedroom
2. Toilet
3. Living room /
   Dining room
4. Kitchen
5. Inside-out
6. Laundry
7. Terrace

## 134

The color and material of walls play an important role in how much of the sun's energy is absorbed and reflected. Dark colors absorb heat, while light colors reflect it.

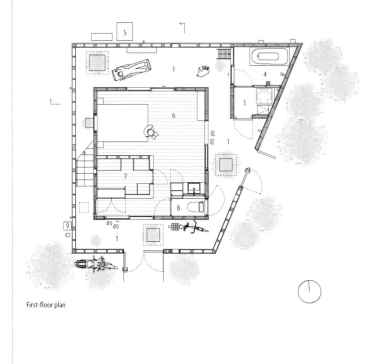

First-floor plan

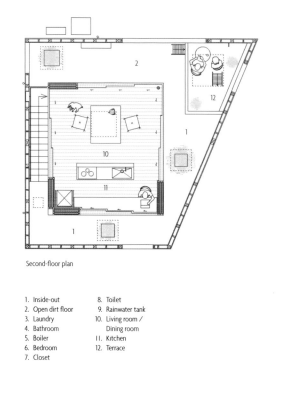

Second-floor plan

1. Inside-out
2. Open dirt floor
3. Laundry
4. Bathroom
5. Boiler
6. Bedroom
7. Closet
8. Toilet
9. Rainwater tank
10. Living room /
    Dining room
11. Kitchen
12. Terrace

## 135

Courtyards are popular in parts of the world with dry and hot climates. Interior courtyards are used as climate control design solutions helping air circulation and allowing light into the interior of a house.

## 136

Trees and plants complement
a courtyard and provide
humidity.

The inner walls of this house can slide to open spaces to the courtyard. The cool air of the courtyard is sheltered from the sun by the exterior walls and roof.

## Herzliya Green House

Architects: Sharon Neuman
Architects
Location: Herzliya, Israel
Photography: © Sharon Neuman
Architects

This house in Herzliya is located on a long, narrow plot with an adjacent building to the west that blocks light and airflow. To deal with this situation, the architects planned a series of staggered blocks creating an irregular eastern façade. This strategy provided south and north light and natural ventilation. In contrast, the eastern wall has few openings.

Cross-section

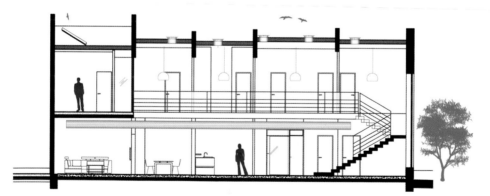

Longitudinal section

## 137

A passive design approach can involve the structure of a building; including orientation, window and skylight placement, insulation, and building materials.

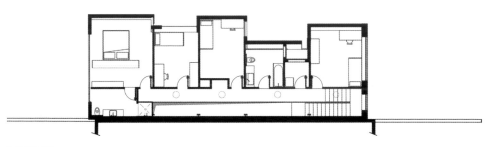

Second-floor plan

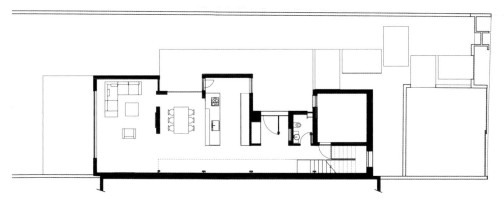

First-floor plan

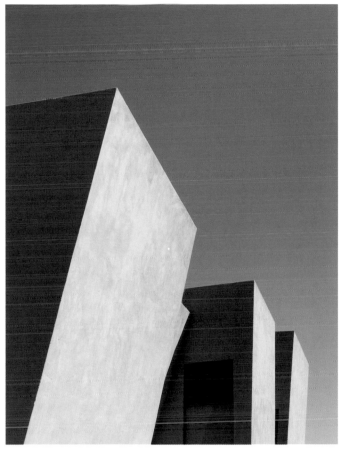
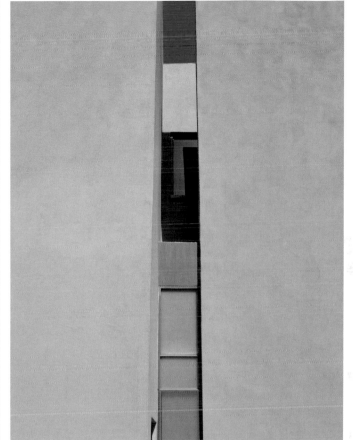

The house incorporates adobe blocks in specific places for extra thermal mass, a solar water heater, and a rainwater collecting system.

## 138

Window geometry, size, and disposition can influence indoor lighting. Taller windows give greater penetrations and wider windows offer a better distribution of light.

## 139

Slanted windows allow natural light in without the glare and summer solar gain. This makes the interior less dependent on artificial light and allows for energy conservation.

Aside from the aesthetic value, the all-white surfaces of this interior combined with good lighting, maximize the potential of the architectural features.

## 140

The careful management of natural and artificial light can generate important energy savings, while preventing glare and minimizing heat gains.

### Thomas Eco-House

Architects: Dan Nelson AIA,
Matt Radach/Designs
Northwest Architects
Location: Stanwood, WA, USA
Photography: © Lucas Henning

This four-story home allows a large amount of living space, while maintaining
a relatively small carbon footprint; it also takes advantage of the views that the site
has to offer. The design process of the house was guided by the owner's interest in
energy efficiency and a sustainable, low-maintenance design. The site is landscaped
with native vegetation; it is irrigated in the dry summer months with rainwater runoff
from the roof that is stored in a cistern.

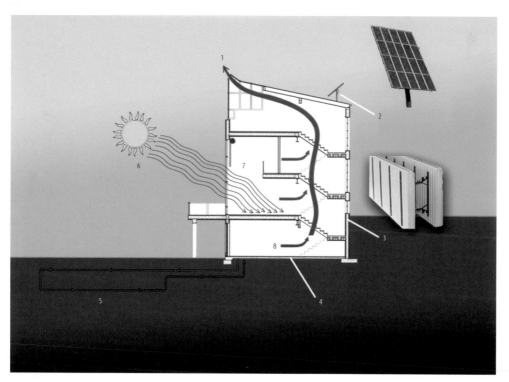

Sustainable strategies diagram

1. Solar chimney for natural
   ventilation
2. Wired for solar
3. Insulated concrete for walls
4. Radiant floor heat
5. Geothermal heating
6. Passive solar
7. Motorized solar shade
8. Concrete floor solar mass

# 141

A sustainable home design
is successful when every
component, including
structure, mechanical
equipment, and materials
used, is linked to produce
a single organism.

142

Light-colored interiors
and open-floor plans optimize
the use of artificial lighting
in a sustainable manner.

## 143

ICF (insulated concrete form) is a wall assembly with insulation layers on both the interior and exterior sides, creating a very efficient and airtight wall system.

## 144

In home design, light and
ventilation requirements
determine the size of windows
and whether they have to
be operable or fixed based
on a percentage of the floor
area of a habitable space.

North elevation

West elevation

South elevation

East elevation

Main floor plan

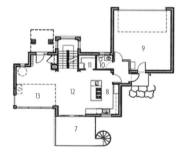

"Bubble" floor plan

1. Media room
2. Family room
3. Bedroom
4. Bathroom
5. Mechanical room
6. Laundry
7. Deck
8. Kitchen
9. Garage
10. Toilet
11. Pantry
12. Dining room
13. Living room
14. Master bedroom
15. Closet
16. Loft
17. "Bubble"
18. Roof deck

Lower floor plan

Upper floor plan

In order to improve efficiency for heating and cooling, the house uses a geothermal heat pump tied in with a hydronic heating system that absorbs heat from the ground.

The glassed-in space atop the staircase has operable windows that, when opened, create a natural convection effect, pulling warm air up the staircase and out of the house.

## Mooloomba House

Architects: Shaun Lockyer
Architects

Location: Point Lookout,
Australia

Photography: © Scott Burrows

This house consists of a series of distinct pavilions around an east-facing courtyard. The courtyard breaks down the scale of the house and opens the spaces up to the easterly breezes. It draws the sun in and creates a private refuge from an adjacent public walkway. The house is set back from the street and its exterior spaces are landscaped so that with time, the boundary will be completely blurred, offering a dense, green edge to the public.

The use of hardwoods, graying cedar,
fiber-cement, and playful colors
reference the local community
in a contemporary fashion.

## 145

It is important to optimize heat gain during the cold months, while keeping it to a minimum in the summer. Exterior shutters are highly efficient in this respect.

Elevations

## 146

Make the most of outdoor living with breezeways and screens that protect patios and terraces from prevailing wind and sunlight.

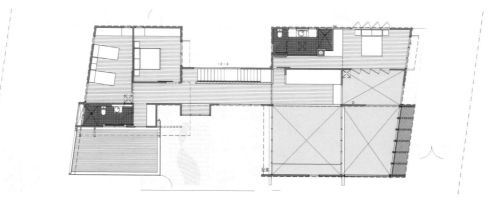

Second-floor plan

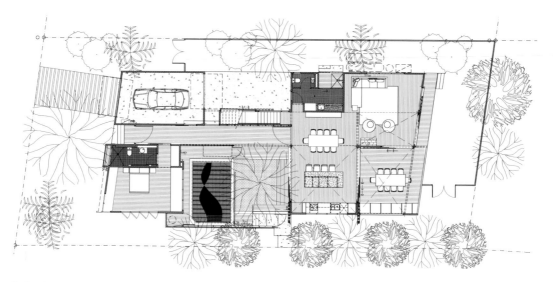

First-floor plan

## 147

The thermal advantages of courtyards are considerable. Courtyards act as cool air containers in the summer and are wind protected exterior spaces in winter.

A slow-combustion stove provides economical heating in winter. Low-E glass, additional insulation, and FSC timbers have been used to bolster the performance of the house.

## 148

Louvered glass windows have evolved over time to have better designs and mechanisms that allow for air tightness. Glass blades can be replaced with wood and aluminum blades.

## CorManca House

Architects: PAUL CREMOUX studio

Location: Mexico City, Mexico

Photography: © Héctor Armanado Herrera, PCW

Built on a small plot of land, CorManca House is three stories with an interior courtyard and a U-shape terrace on the second floor facing a vertical garden. This vertical garden is used as a temperature and humidity control device, enhancing the microclimate of the residence. While the front of the building, clad in black slate, looks monolithic, the back features blocks of indoor and outdoor spaces articulated to make the most of natural light.

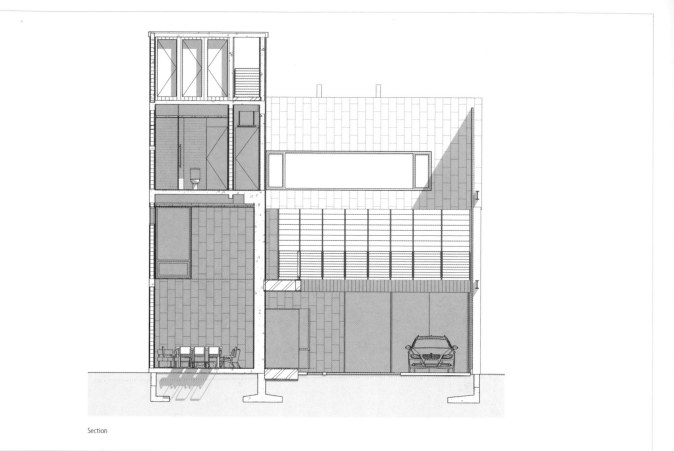

Section

Rendering of front façade

The reduced footprint of the building forced a vertical construction that resulted in a three-story building.

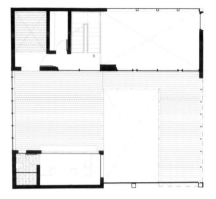

Third-floor plan

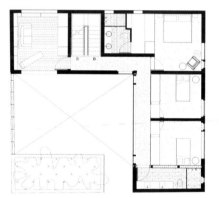

Second-floor plan

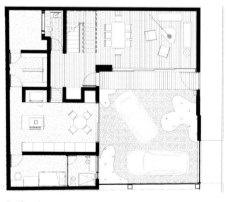

First-floor plan

Concrete and metal framing,
a self-resistant caustic and thermal
tle beam, and a concrete small vault
form the structure of CorManca
House. Finishes include low-VOC
paint and recyclable materials.

## 149

Vertical gardens are effective bio-filters, absorbing volatile organic compounds. They also contribute to cooling a home in the summer and adding humidity to the air during the dry cold months of winter.

The terrace on the second floor compensates for the lack of a larger ground-floor courtyard. It is the focal area around which the house is organized and plays a social role.

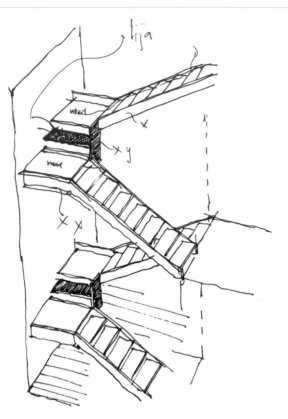

Hand-drawn sketch of staircase

Partial axonometric view of the house

# 150

An open staircase acts as a chimneystack, allowing air to rise to warm upper floors during the winter and vent through windows at the top during the summer.

The dark slate wall captures solar energy
and keeps interior rooms warm.

# Directory

**123DV Modern Villas**
Rotterdam, the Netherlands
www.123DV.nl

**ÁBATON Architects**
Pozuelo de Alarcón, Spain
www.abaton.es

**André Eisenlohr**
Campos do Jordão, Brazil
www.andreeisenlohr.blogspot.com

**Andrew Maynard Architects**
Victoria, Australia
www.maynardarchitects.com.au

**Aroma Italiano**
San José, Costa Rica
www.aromaitaliano.cr

**Atelier d'Architecture Christian Girard**
Paris, France
www.atelierchristiangirard.com

**Austin Patterson Disston Architects**
Southport, CT, USA
www.apdarchitects.com

**Bob Burnett Architecture**
Christchurch, New Zealand
www.bbarc.com

**Brooks + Scarpa**
Los Angeles, CA, USA
www.brooksscarpa.com

**ColectivoMX**
Mexico City, Mexico
www.colectivomx.com.mx

**Design for Occupancy**
Portland, OR, USA
www.designforoccupancy.net

**Designs Northwest Architects**
Stanwood, WA, USA
www.designsnw.com

**Dorrington Architects & Associates**
Auckland, New Zealand
www.dorringtonarchitects.co.nz

**Edward Fitzgerald / Architects**
Albuquerque, NM, USA
www.efarchitects.com

**EFTYCHIS**
Johannesburg, South Africa
www.eftychis.com

**Egeon Architecten**
Amsterdam, the Netherlands
www.egeon.eu

**Fernanda Vuillemier**
Puerto Natales, Chile
www.fernandavuillemier.com

**Grzywinski+Pons**
New York, NY, USA
www.gp-arch.com

**Hays + Ewing Design Studio**
Charlottesville, VA, USA
www.hays-ewing.com

**HUF HAUS**
Hartenfels, Germany
www.huf-haus.com

**James & Mau**
Madrid, Spain
Santiago, Chile
Bogotá, Colombia
www.jamesandmau.com

Kjellgren Kaminsky Architecture
Göteborg, Sweden
www.kjellgrenkaminsky.se

Malka Architects
Haifa, Israel
www.malka-arch.com

Minarc
Santa Monica, CA, USA
www.minarc.com

MODERNest
Toronto, ON, Canada
www.modernest.ca

Neil M. Denari Architects
Los Angeles, CA, USA
www.nmda-inc.com

Paul Archer Design
London, United Kingdom
www.paularcherdesign.co.uk

PAUL CREMOUX studio
Mexico City, Mexico
www.paulcremoux.com

Philipp Architekten
Untermünkheim, Germany
www.philipp-architekten.de

Powerhouse Company
Rotterdam, the Netherlands
Copenhagen, Denmark
Shanghai, China
www.powerhouse-company.com

RAU
Amsterdam, the Netherlands
www.rau.eu

Seeley Architects
Torquay, Australia
www.seeleyarchitects.com.au

Sharon Neuman Architects
Caesarea, Israel
www.sharon-neuman.co.il

Shaun Lockyer Architects
Fortitude Valley, Brisbane, Australia
www.lockyerarchitects.com.au

Silva Studios Architecture
San Diego, CA, USA
www.silvastudios.com

Stelle Lomont Rouhani Architects
New York, NY, USA
www.stelleco.com

Studio 804
Lawrence, KS, USA
www.studio804.com

Takeshi Hosaka Architects
Yokohama, Japan
www.hosakatakeshi.com

Taylor & Miller
New York, NY, USA
www.taylorandmiller.com

Utopia Arquitectura e Engenharia
Porto, Portugal
www.utopia-projects.com

Zimmerman and Associates
Sausalito and Sonoma, CA, USA
www.zmanarch.com